Peaceful Transition

Conscious Dying: The process of maintaining a connection between the soul and the Higher Self at the moment of physical death in order to assure the soul's arrival at the soul plane without the interference of disorienting forces of the karmic cycle. This technique may result in the immediate liberation of the soul from the need to reincarnate.

LIBERATE YOUR SOUL

We all know that we can choose to improve the way we live, but can we choose to improve the way we die? Dr. Bruce Goldberg says yes, and that, by doing so, we can ascend to the higher planes and liberate our souls from the bondage of karma.

To die without losing consciousness is the very essence of enlightenment and immortality. History is full of references to conscious dying, including the *Tibetan* and *Egyptian Books of the Dead*, the Greek Mystery Schools, even the Bible. Ancient disciplines taught that if the soul could maintain a connection with its perfect counterpart (the Higher Self) at the moment of death, eternal bliss would be its reward.

There are many benefits to conscious dying: you can shorten your karmic cycle (resulting in fewer remaining lifetimes), while you increase the quality of your remaining lifetimes; in this lifetime you will enjoy instant recall of past lives, along with an increase in your psychic abilities; and you will experience tremendous spiritual growth, shattering your fear of death forever.

This book introduces two unique concepts and techniques. One is "cleansing" and the other is the Conscious Out-of-Body Experience (COBE). You will learn what to think, feel, say, and how to behave at the moment of death. You will read actual case histories of patients who have successfully used these techniques, and you will have the opportunity to practice the conscious dying technique through self-hypnosis and meditation exercises.

In the tenth book of *The Republic* Plato said, "practice dying." Now you can practice dying so that you may perfect living.

ABOUT THE AUTHOR

Dr. Bruce Goldberg holds a B.A. degree in Biology and Chemistry, is a Doctor of Dental Surgery, and has an M.S. degree in Counseling Psychology. He retired from dentistry in 1989, and has concentrated on his hypnotherapy practice in Los Angeles. Dr. Goldberg was trained by the American Society of Clinical Hypnosis in the techniques and clinical applications of hypnosis.

Dr. Goldberg has been interviewed on the Donahue, Oprah, Joan Rivers, The Other Side, Regis and Kathie Lee, Tom Snyder, Jerry Springer, Jenny Jones, and Montel Williams shows, by CNN, CBS News, and many others.

Through lectures, television and radio appearances, and newspaper articles, including interviews in *TIME, The Los Angeles Times,* and *The Washington Post*, Dr. Goldberg has educated many people in the benefits of hypnosis. He has conducted more than 33,000 past life regressions and future life progressions since 1974, helping thousands of patients empower themselves through these techniques. His cassette tapes teach people self-hypnosis, and guide them into past and future lives. He gives lectures and seminars on hypnosis, regression and progression therapy, and conscious dying; he is a also a consultant to corporations, attorneys, and the local and network media. His first edition of *The Search for Grace* was made into a television movie by CBS. His third book, *Soul Healing*, is a classic on alternative medicine and psychic empowerment. Dr. Goldberg's column "Hypnotic Highways" appears in *FATE* magazine.

Dr. Goldberg distributes cassette tapes to teach people self-hypnosis and to guide them into past and future lives. For information on self-hypnosis tapes, speaking engagements, or private sessions, Dr. Goldberg can be contacted directly by writing to:

Bruce Goldberg, D.D.S., M.S.
4300 Natoma Avenue
Woodland Hills, CA 91364
Telephone: (800) KARMA-4-U or (800) 527-6248
Fax: (818) 704-9189
Please include a self-addressed, stamped envelope with your letter.

By the Author of *Past Lives—Future Lives*

Peaceful Transition

DR.
BRUCE
GOLDBERG

The Art of Conscious Dying & the Liberation of the Soul

1997
Llewellyn Publications
St. Paul, Minnesota 55164-0383, U.S.A.

FIRST EDITION
First Printing, 1997

Cover design by Tom Grewe
Cover photo from Stock Photo
Editing and interior design by Connie Hill

Library of Congress Cataloging-in-Publication Data
Goldberg, Bruce, 1948–
    Peaceful transition : the art of conscious dying and the liberation of the soul / by Bruce Goldberg
      p. cm. --
    Includes bibliographical references and index.
    ISBN 1–56718–319–0 (pbk.)
    1. Death—Religious aspects. 2. Spiritual life. 3. Soul. I. Title.
BL325.D35G64   1997
291.2'3—dc21   97-20431
                                              CIP

Quotations from the Compendium of the *Theological and Spiritual Writings of Emanuel Swedenborg* are used with the permission of the Swedenborg Foundation, West Chester, PA. The reproduction of the detail of the "Ascent into the Empyrium" from *Visions of the Hereafter* by Hieronymus Bosch is used with permission by arrangement with Alinari/Art Resource, New York.

Llewellyn Worldwide does not participate in, endorse, or have any authority or responsibility concerning private business transactions between our authors and the public.

All mail addressed to the author is forwarded but the publisher cannot, unless specifically instructed by the author, give out an address or phone number.

Llewellyn Publications
A Division of Llewellyn Worldwide, Ltd.
St. Paul, Minnesota 55164-0383, U.S.A.

ACKNOWLEDGMENTS

I would like to express my consciously undying gratitude to the Eastern Sages, Dr. Raymond Moody (a friend and colleague) and all of the researchers in Near Death Experiences, and the thousands of patients I have had the pleasure to train in spiritual empowerment and conscious dying. In addition, I am indebted to the quantum physicists who have placed this entire field of parapsychology on firm ground.

OTHER BOOKS BY DR. BRUCE GOLDBERG

Past Lives—Future Lives
The Search for Grace: The True Story of Murder and Reincarnation
Soul Healing

Forthcoming

Look Younger, Live Longer: Add 20 to 50 Quality Years to Your Life
New Age Hypnosis
Protected by the Light: The Complete Book of Psychic Self-Defense
The Ultimate Truth
Astral Voyages: Mastering the Art of Soul Travel

CONTENTS

NOTE TO THE READER

At times, the masculine form has been used as a convention. It is intended to imply both male and female genders where this is applicable.

Some of the minor details in the case histories have been altered to protect the privacy of my patients. All of the names used, except the celebrities mentioned, have been altered. Everything else in these pages is true.

FOREWORD

This is a guidebook for the living—before, during, and after they undergo that part of the process of living that is incorrectly referred to as "dying." It is intended for use by all, irrespective of their religious inclinations or beliefs.

This book's main purpose is to help the individual go through the process of dying without losing consciousness. To die consciously seems to be the very essence of both immortality and liberation of the soul or enlightenment—the ultimate form of empowerment. This book is also intended to assist in maintaining the integrity and continuity of consciousness after dying, through the intermediate state between death and rebirth, and through the process of being reborn.

This book has one main theme: Conscious Dying is the key that will unlock the door to the elimination of the karmic cycle and the ascension of the soul to heaven, nirvana, or whatever the individual's belief system refers to as its ultimate destiny. This system will even work with atheists.

To prevent the loss of consciousness at the moment of death will bring about a spiritual "cleansing." Cleansing is the ability to go through death consciously, through birth consciously, between death and rebirth consciously, reconstituting the broken thread of consciousness through all the major alterations of consciousness and helping restore the integrity of humankind's true being. It thus results in a liberation from the cycle of birth and death, also known as the karmic cycle. This cleansing is also referred to as a conscious out-of-body experience (COBE).

What to think, what to feel, what to say, and how to behave at the moment of death principally, but also before and after it, is what this book will show you. A documented case history of a patient who has successfully used these techniques will be presented, and I have included exercises for the reader in Part II so that they may use this book as a guidebook for their own transition. By reading and applying the principles and techniques prescribed in this book, you will gain enormous insight into the most perplexing problem facing humankind. That enigma is how to free the soul from the tedious and painful cycle of death and rebirth.

This guidebook has three main purposes. First, it is a technique manual on the art of dying. Second, it is a book offering empowerment for the dying and his or her loved ones. Last, the book describes the experiences of the deceased during the intermediate period of their transition, and instructs the soul in regard to this voyage. It is a form of traveler's guide to other worlds.

Many people practice golf, play tennis, use their computers, and play a musical instrument. People do not practice dying—they just die, and this is what I refer to as unconscious dying. Ignorance of the metaphysical concepts involved is the main reason that we do not practice dying.

I honestly feel that if the average person was made aware of conscious dying and its many advantages over unconscious dying, this book would not be necessary. The sad fact is that this compilation is needed to educate the public to assist them in their own liberation.

History is full of references to conscious dying. The New Testament, especially 1 Corinthians, gives further evidence of this discipline:

Flesh and blood cannot inherit the Kingdom of God.

We shall not all sleep, but we shall all be changed.

In a moment, in the twinkling of an eye, at the last trumpet: for the trumpet shall sound and the dead shall be raised incorruptible, and we shall be changed.

For this corruptible must put on incorruption and this mortal must put on immortality.

So when this corruptible shall have put on incorruption, and this mortal shall have put on immortality, then shall be brought to pass the saying that is written, Death is swallowed up in victory.[1]

A more detailed historical account of conscious dying is given in Part III.

The simple solution to this soul's liberation was given by Plato when he instructed, "practice dying." We can practice dying by learning how to die without losing consciousness. The techniques given in chapter 10 are rather comprehensive and include both meditation and self-hypnosis examples. Daily use of these disciplines will be more than enough preparation for your eventual transition.

Our main problem comes from the way we think. We live in a world where ignorance and misunderstanding dominate. Some say we function as three separate people. The first is who we think we are. Second is who others think we are. Who we really are is the third aspect.

The first two parts make up our ego: the basis of our dysfunctional thinking, feeling, and behavior. The ego is the creation of the conscious mind (defense mechanism). The "unthought self" (the true self) is created by the God energy. This unthought self is our subconscious mind (soul), especially in its connection to the superconscious mind (Higher Self), which is an extension of the God energy. That is why it is so important to maintain this connection at the moment of physical death, hence conscious dying.

---

1   St. Paul. 1 Corinthians 15:51–56.

For those of you who disagree and think that the ego is a perfect replication of who you really are, consider this. Would you be empowered and happy if this ego were some type of illusionary identity projected into a temporary and mind-created physical existence?

Science adds fuel to this ignorance. It is unable to liberate itself from its conditioned consciousness and officially certifies this false identification through intellectual, empirical, and materialistic doctrines. None of these principles pass the reality tests that are well established by quantum physics. This new physics demonstrates that it is the consciousness or subconscious mind that actually creates reality.

This illusion of identification with the physical body is considered scientific fact by Western science. As part of this illusion the public is brainwashed to think:

- There is no soul.

- Only physical life exists. There is no after-life.

- Consciousness is a component of the physical brain and ceases to exist when the body dies.

It is only through awareness and knowledge that we can defeat this ignorance. Socrates said, "Knowledge is virtue." "Knowledge is power," was uttered by Francis Bacon. Jesus said, "Ye shall know the truth, and the truth shall make you free." I can think of no other human condition where this truth is more needed than at the moment of death.

We can remove this fear and ignorance by practicing conscious dying. We can prepare ourselves for a beautiful, spiritually empowering, and peaceful transition. We can attain this liberation of the soul. Pierre Teilhard de Chardin, following the thought of St. Paul, and motivated by his philosophy of spiritual evolution, which he called Christogenesis, thought of man at the Omega Point of Evolution, the end of the evolutionary process, at which one becomes Christified and attains liberation or perfection.

There are several advantages to using the principles and techniques presented in this book. Among those are an understanding of:

- The laws of karma.

- The actual process of dying.

- The laws of thought and consciousness and how they operate.

- How not to be afraid of death and dying.

- How not to lose consciousness at the moment of death and rebirth.

- How to call on spiritual guides and one's own higher self for help.

- The true nature of a human being.

- The true nature of death.

- How not to identify with the mind-emotion process.

- How not to identify with the physical body.

- How not to identify with the ego.

- How to free oneself from the karmic cycle.

Part I

The Art and Science of Conscious Dying

...death is not an ending for life
or a cause for fear,
but a necessary transition—
a peaceful transition

CHAPTER 1

What Is Conscious Dying?

The concept of death suggest two time-honored questions. The first is: "How can I avoid death?" The second question is: "How can I accept death and die without fear?" It is this latter goal that we will take up in this book.

The fact that birth and death occur many times in a soul's evolution is common knowledge to those who subscribe to Buddhist philosophy. Actually our dying and being replaced occur every moment of our lives. Modern science informs us that every cell in our physical structure has been replaced at least once every nine months.

We will all experience death eventually. Knowing how to traverse this dimensional shift correctly requires enlightenment and has many advantages for the spiritually evolved soul. The Ancient Mystery Schools, along with the *Tibetan Book of the Dead*, clearly stated that the unenlightened do not fare well with this transition and repress all knowledge of their past lives. Both these ancient disciplines taught that if the soul could somehow maintain a connection with its perfect counterpart (Higher Self) at the moment of death, eternal bliss would be its reward. I call this connection conscious dying (conscious out-of-body experience, or COBE).

CHAPTER 1

A human's senses are decisively limited. There are sounds we cannot hear, feelings we cannot feel, objects we cannot see, and tastes we cannot taste. We assume our ego is our only consciousness, but there are other consciousnesses, acknowledged by psychology and the new physics, and demonstrated by yogins and saints. Merely because we do not comprehend something does not mean it is nonexistent. Does it sound so far-fetched that the Ancient Eastern disciples of yoga and meditation, for example, may assist us in the West to find this missing part of the consciousness enigma? As we shall see later on in this book, the new physics mathematically demonstrates these concepts.

By opening ourselves up to what the ancients have known all along, Western science will attain at-one-ment with Eastern science. The transition to what we call death can and should be accompanied by solemn joyousness—a peaceful transition. By practicing conscious dying, the fear of death will be overcome and the soul will be truly empowered.

One soul may assist another in this transition. The Moslem's Fatiha, the Pretashraddha of Hinduism, and the Requiem Mass in Catholicism are modern examples of attempts at conscious dying

The dying should face death not only calmly, clear-mindedly, and heroically, but with an intellect rightly trained, rightly directed, and spiritually transcending soul. This is possible if they have practiced efficiently during their active lifetime the art of conscious dying. But in the West where this technique is little known and rarely practiced, there is, contrastingly, a common unwillingness to die.

With the aid of psychology, the rationalizing mind of the West has pushed forward into what one might call metaphysical neuroticism, and has been brought to an inevitable standstill by the uncritical assumption that everything psychological is subjective and personal.

I submit that humankind invented death in an attempt to identify with the ego's defense mechanisms. A separate ego only exists in our mind. The new physics tells us that we create our reality. Conscious dying shows us how to uncreate the death experience. How can we be dead if we are experiencing conscious dying?

Death represents the unknown; it is so greatly feared, yet so little understood. We are all aware that one day this moment of death will be upon us. It is unavoidable, is it not?

Life is continual and eternal; death may be viewed as the door of transition that leads from one form of life to another, or from the completion of one phase of living to the beginning of still another phase of living. Death is as natural a phenomenon as birth; in a sense, they are one, both making way for the renewal and continuation of life.

The new physics shows us that the entire universe is in a continuous state of flux. Our current life is but a fleeting moment in an infinite flow of reality and consciousness. The purpose of this appears to be our continued growth and spiritual evolution!

We only need to take a closer look at nature, or even our own physical body, to dispel the fear that death is complete annihilation, for nothing is ever completely destroyed, but rather recycled for renewal. The spirit or individuality of all living things return to the form again and again; with each return, the spirit within strives for the perfecting of the form.

There is a universal deathlessness for the spirit of all things. The phenomenon of recurrence or repetition, of which we see so many instances in nature: the waking and the sleeping in the seasons, the inbreathing and the outbreathing of all life forms, can all be attributed to reincarnation.

When we believe that life is essentially independent of the body we inhabit, then failure of the body cannot mean life's extinction, for the individual is a mental being as well, and can pass into a different state of being. There is the same consciousness, with all its emotions and impressions and images the individual has formed over a lifetime—his or her memory contains all of these. The after-death is a state of withdrawal from the contacts, conditions, and scenes with which we are familiar, but this period of rest does not represent a cessation of life.

We need to find meaning at the time of death, when life seems to no longer have a purpose. Our death can and does have meaning in that it results in a new life for us all. In observing the cyclic process of nature, we can see the logic behind the idea that death is only part of the complete cycle of earthly life and the after death, that life is eternal and perpetual. The natural law of constant renewal demonstrates that for every period of activity there follows a period of rest.

It is necessary for us to accept the visible evidence that death is inevitable for all of us, but should not be feared, as the evidence also implies that death is a necessary event in nature's/God's plan. We do not fear the night, as we know with certainty that it will be followed by the day—in fact, we look forward to the night, for we know it represents a period of rest from our long day's activities.

It is important to remember that the basic teaching of most religions of the world is that the human soul is immortal and indestructible. Human misinterpretation of this basic teaching may leave one feeling that he or she has but one life to live.

It is only in man's earthly sojourn that he forgets that he is an immortal soul, and lives rather in the illusion that he is only his physical body; of course, the truth is that he is an immortal spirit and soul dwelling or living in a temporary body.

We become so engrossed with the earthly and material matter that we forget our own true identity as an immortal soul. When we are able to see ourselves as immortal souls inhabiting bodies as vehicles for growth, via experience, we can then become aware of our greater purpose in life, and truly know our physical body for what it is really is— a temple of the soul and a path to God.

The soul seeks the necessary opportunities for its greater growth through reincarnation and its learning experiences. While resting between lifetimes, the soul assimilates the lessons of its previous life and, upon assessment and review of the needs yet to be met, the soul will again set out to accomplish these new goals on the physical plane. With each succeeding life, we achieve greater awareness of our purpose for living, and will, after many incarnations, outgrow our need for embodiment into the physical level. We will then enter the higher levels of existence permanently.

If our ties with people are of a selfless love—remembering that love is the strongest force in the universe—then the time of their death is a time to show this selfless love by putting away our suffering and longing so as not to hold the departed one back, but rather to release and bless this one on his or her new journey. When we can feel secure in the knowledge that the ties of love are never broken, it will be easier for us to release ourselves from mourning and suffering, and from the assumption that the relationship is permanently dissolved. It is time also for us to realize that death is not an ending for life or a cause for fear, but a necessary transition—a peaceful transition.

Our understanding of death rests in the death of our ego. The real you (soul) is eternal. It cannot die. If we believe in classical death paradigms we are giving power to this false hypothesis.

When we discuss conscious dying, there are certain terms that must be understood in order to comprehend this concept. Throughout this book I will refer to these ideas and expand upon them, but for now I would like to establish these basic definitions.

The *conscious mind* is divided into two main components. One part is termed the conscious mind proper and consists of our analytical, critical, and basic left-brain activities. This part of our mind literally dies when the physical body crosses into spirit, so it is not relevant to our discussion.

The other component of our consciousness is our *subconscious mind* (soul or spirit), which is our creative, emotional, and right-brain function. This subconscious is pure energy in the form of electromagnetic radiation, and it is indestructible. It is what reincarnates into a new body when the physical body dies; it is our soul. Although it may be pure energy, it is far from perfect. The main purpose of reincarnation via the karmic cycle is to perfect the soul.

The *superconscious mind* or *Higher Self* is the perfect part of the subconscious mind. The Higher Self comes from the God plane and advises us on how to perfect the subconscious. When we do eventually achieve this ideal, our subconscious merges with the Higher Self and ascends to the higher planes (see chapter 3).

Cleansing is the technique of introducing the subconscious to the Higher Self so that a connection results. This connection will allow the Higher Self to raise the quality of the subconscious mind's energy (frequency vibrational rate) to a higher and more perfect level. This is the main technique I use with my patients in my Los Angeles office to train them to grow spiritually and to become immune to issues to which they were previously vulnerable. I also call this a superconscious mind tap.

This cleansing mechanism is also the key to conscious dying. By maintaining this connection between the soul and its Higher Self, the soul can learn to repeat this technique at the moment of death. This will result in the soul avoiding the disorienting forces of the karmic cycle that block out all memories of previous lives and make it nearly impossible for a soul to adapt to the world in its new body in a spiritually positive and growth-oriented manner.

Near-death experiences (NDEs) will be fully discussed in chapter 2, but for our current purpose let us refer to it as unconscious dying. The main difference between an NDE and death itself is that in the former the recipient lives to talk about it. NDEs are actually a form of death, but for such a short time that it is reversible.

There is no connection made between the subconscious and Higher Self during this time. This thread of continuity that is so critical for conscious dying is simply missing. We refer to an NDE as unconscious dying for that very reason.

NDEs represent one form of *out-of-body experiences* (OBEs). The other types of OBE do not require physical death for a brief time. Runners' hypnosis, dreams, and reverie states, drug-induced states and the mind's response to extremely stressful situations are common examples of OBEs (see chapter 9). All OBEs are perfectly safe—it is only the NDE that may result in actual physical death. These states are also referred to as altered states of consciousness (ASCs). I will use the term conscious out-of-body experience (COBE) to refer to conscious dying.

The *soul plane* is the dimension we go to in between lives to evaluate our most recent lifetime and decide upon our next sojourn. We will discuss this in greater detail in chapters 3 and 12.

CONSCIOUS DYING TODAY

To die, or cross into spirit, consciously, is to face clinical death without the loss of continuity of one's consciousness. This is the very essence of enlightenment and immortality. It is the only true path to liberation from the karmic cycle, or from the need to reincarnate over and over again until perfection is achieved.

At the moment of death our physical body clinically dies (including the ego), but our subconscious mind (soul) survives. If it can maintain direct contact with its perfect energy counterpart (superconscious mind or Higher Self) at this time, it will literally die consciously, the soul (subconscious mind) will be liberated, and spiritual growth will result.

However, if this contact is not maintained (unconscious death) then our soul will have missed a great opportunity for enlightenment and the most uncomfortable characteristics (the disorienting forces) of the karmic cycle will prevail.

Since the subconscious and superconscious mind (Higher Self) are actually energy, they cannot be destroyed. The first law of thermodynamics in physics clearly states that energy cannot be destroyed, merely altered in its form. For example, light can be transformed into electrical energy or heat, but the total amount of energy we end up with in this new form must equal that of the light at the start of the process.

The subconscious and Higher Self are, in reality, electromagnetic radiation. This harmless type of radiation is what comprises a television or radio signal.

To return to the concept of conscious dying, I refer you to Figure 1 (page 10). Please note that the God energy overviews the entire process. The soul plane is where the soul goes between lifetimes to decide on its next life (see chapter 3 and 12).

From the soul plane, most souls will experience the disorienting forces of the lower planes (more on the plane concept in chapter 3) and goes through an unconscious rebirth into a physical body. All memories of its previous lives and its gestation on the soul plane will, for the most part, be lost. Throughout physical life consciousness is evident. Note the dotted lines that lead to altered states of consciousness (ASC). One form of ASC is an OBE (out-of-body experience). Note how the soul can leave and return from this experience.

The NDE (near-death experience) requires the body to literally die for a period from a few seconds to several minutes long. The NDE will result in either returning to the physical body or to actual death itself.

From clinical death, you will note that the solid line returns to the disorienting forces of the lower planes. Then the Higher Self guides the subconscious back to the soul plane to choose its next lifetime. This is unconscious dying.

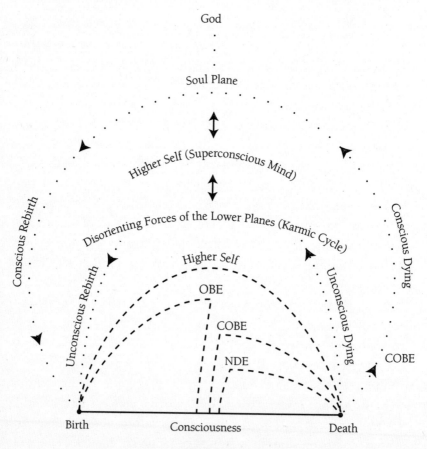

Figure 1
The Conscious Dying Process

The conscious dying process is illustrated by COBE (conscious out-of-body experience), during which our soul is carried through the death experience and avoids the karmic cycle on its return to the soul plane. When this liberated soul (subconscious mind) is reborn, it again avoids the karmic cycle interference and the conscious rebirth process is complete.

What is doing all of this traveling is the subconscious mind (soul). The Higher Self advises it and is also present throughout physical life. The Higher Self is especially pronounced on the soul plane. Note that the Higher Self is able to go to and from the soul plane, as indicated by the arrows going in both directions.

It is easy to see the many advantages that conscious dying has over the typical unconscious dying. Some of these advantages are:

- Shortening of our karmic cycle. This results in fewer remaining lifetimes.

- An increase in the quality of the remaining life.

- An instant recall of all past lives.

- Empowerment.

- Tremendous spiritual growth.

- An increase in psychic abilities.

- The elimination of the fear of death.

- Shorter bereavement (grief) experience for the loved ones left behind.

- An increase in the quality of the universe as a whole.

One of the main advantages in experiencing conscious dying is in discovering that the world beyond earth is merely another dimension of existence. It is a kind of "spiritual oasis" that nurtures and guides the soul as it continues to evolve higher in its return to the source from whence it came.

CHAPTER 2

Near-Death Experiences

The best scientific evidence of the soul's survival beyond the physical death of the body are near-death experiences (NDEs). Depictions of NDEs have been around for a long time. Dr. Raymond Moody, in his ground-breaking book *Life After Life*, coined the term "near-death experience."[1]

Rod Serling wrote a *Twilight Zone* episode that aired fifteen years before Moody's book appeared in print. In this episode, Jack Klugman played the role of an unhappy cynical trumpet player who felt he had no reason to live. He walks in front of a moving car and has an NDE. During this time he meets the angel Gabriel and is engaged in a long philosophical discussion about life and death. When Klugman finally does declare that he has something to live for, he is returned to his physical body unharmed.

The message here is that when we need help this aid is available if we ask for it. As a society we have become more aware of this phenomenon since Dr. Moody's book first appeared in 1975. Researchers may differ somewhat in their specific conclusions about NDE, but their

---

1 Dr. Raymond Moody, *Life After Life* (New York: Bantam Books, 1975).

studies reveal a similar picture of this phenomenon. The typical encounter is described as being in a dream. Surprisingly, this experience seems more real than ordinary waking consciousness. The five senses are heightened; thought processes are rational and crystal clear.

The main difference noted is a disconnectedness from your physical body. A floating sensation ensues and the soul views the lifeless body from a corner of the ceiling. A sense of calm and serenity dominates now, and time has no meaning. The soul feels drawn to a dark tunnel with a brilliant white light at its end.

As you enter the white light, a loved one or a religious figure greets you. At this time you become aware that you will return to your physical body. Prior to this, however, you have perceived in the form of flashbacks an instantaneous panoramic review of your former life.

Most people do not remember these events when they are resuscitated. Some people report becoming aware of discomfort or being propelled uncontrollably back into their body. Reports prevail of a greater appreciation of life, an increase in the importance of personal relationships, and a determination to maximize the opportunities afforded to them.

In summary, the core experience of an NDE includes (1) hearing loud noises very early in the death process; (2) moving through a long, dark tunnel; (3) seeing a white or gold light that is separate from oneself; (4) seeing religious figures like Jesus or Buddha or Moses; (5) a panoramic life review/judgment; and (6) indications that this is a learning process.

It must be pointed out that any NDE represents only the early stage of death. *The Tibetan Book of the Dead* (see chapter 19) would classify this as the first bardo after death.[2] What is interesting is that the death process, like life, involves choice. These choices form the basis for learning as well as the initiation of personal experience.

Children also report NDEs, but their experiences differ. They have more vivid recollections and see the brilliant white light twice as often as adults. Children have shown a tendency to temporarily forego their childhood identities and become "ageless and wise beyond their

---

2   W. Y. Evans-Wentz, *The Tibetan Book of the Dead* (New York: Oxford University Press, 1960).

years." In addition, the panoramic memory life review is absent in a child's NDE.

Kenneth Ring's book, *Life at Death*, reports that forty-eight percent of the people he interviewed who had an NDE described the core experience.[3] Prior religious beliefs had no effect on these observations. In fact, more NDE experiencers than non-experiencers previously felt that death resulted in the end of consciousness. None of Ring's subjects experienced anything hellish. Eighty percent of the subjects reported that they now had little or no fear of death.

Nearly twice as many of those who had no NDEs were aware of this phenomenon and through the media of the work of Elizabeth Kübler-Ross and Raymond Moody's work. This defeats any argument that the experiencers were culturally conditioned to have this result.

Another qualifying factor to these reports being accurate comes from the reports of Michael Sabom, an Atlanta cardiologist. He interviewed thirty-two patients who claimed to have had an NDE. None of them made any major mistakes in describing the resuscitation procedures applied to them while they were out of their body observing these procedures. Sabom noted that twenty-three of twenty-five patients who did not have an NDE, but made "educated guesses" as to the procedures involved, made major errors in their reports to him.[4]

Moody reported that a woman was able to accurately describe the instruments that were employed in her resuscitation following a heart attack—right down to their colors. What makes this case especially significant is that this elderly patient had been blind for fifty years! Moody, among others, also reports a reluctance to return among NDE receivers. Some of these patients even express anger toward their doctors for bringing them back.

One rather interesting observation from some NDE reports is that of precognition. Ring reports a "life preview" and "world preview" as a component of these futuristic depictions.

---

3   Kenneth Ring, *Life at Death: A Scientific Investigation of the Near-Death Experience* (New York: Quill, 1982).

4   Michael Sabom, *Recollections of Death: A Medical Investigation* (New York: Harper & Row, 1982).

The life previews were glimpses of the patient's future, and unique to each individual. However, there was considerable consistency of global events, both in timing and content. The life previews are presented as a vivid memory rather than a forecast, and are highly detailed. They seem to occur as an extension of the panoramic life review.

There is documentation for many of these futuristic projections, according to Ring. One man described the Three Mile Island incident to his wife just two days before it happened. Another patient described the eruption of Mount St. Helens to her husband. He mocked her until a few hours later when this event was shown on their local television news. Since 1977 my work with age progression through hypnosis most definitely demonstrates the accuracy of the mind's ability to see the future. I refer you to my first book, *Past Lives—Future Lives*,[5] for a detailed discussion of progression, along with case histories.

Ring also noted that NDEs resulting from illness were more likely to contain the core experience than those from accidents. On the other hand, the accident experiencers were more likely to experience the panoramic life review as compared to the victims of illness or attempted suicides.

The decision to return is often related to some unfinished business that the patient feels must be completed prior to his or her death.

THE NEAR-DEATH EXPERIENCE THAT INSPIRED DR. RAYMOND MOODY'S WORK

I am fortunate in having had the pleasure of knowing Dr. Raymond Moody since 1983. We were both conducting workshops at an Association of Research and Enlightenment (A.R.E., The Edgar Cayce Foundation) Conference in Washington, D.C.

Ray is also the first person to document the core experience of an NDE. As the father of the field of NDE, his work has added significantly to the field of conscious dying, even though an NDE is an example of unconscious dying.

---

5   Dr. Bruce Goldberg, *Past Lives—Future Lives* (New York: Ballantine, 1988).

What most people are not aware of is the first case Dr. Moody investigated. This case was responsible for him devoting his entire life to the investigation of NDEs.

If you read Moody's *Life After Life*[6] you will note that the book is dedicated to George Ritchie, M.D. In December 1943, the twenty-year-old Ritchie had been pronounced dead by two doctors. He lay cold, covered from head to toe, for nine minutes. He was traveling through another dimension of life. His guide was Jesus Christ. Miraculously, Ritchie returned to his body, shocking everyone present. He would never be the same again—neither would those whose lives he touched.

Only minutes had passed between Ritchie's death and his miraculous revival, but somewhere beyond time he was absorbing the love and wisdom of Jesus Christ. "Here stood a Being that knew everything that I had ever done in my life, for the panorama of my life surrounded us, and yet he totally accepted and loved me," he wrote.

What Ritchie saw convinced him of the existence, not of a rigid judgmental God, but of a God whose love for his creatures is ever-ascending. He saw that a person's learning did not stop with physical death. Endless levels of attainment await us.

A HISTORICAL OVERVIEW OF NDE

There are many references throughout recorded history of what we label today as an NDE. The Old Testament has two interesting references:

Isaiah 26:19: Thy dead men shall live, together with my dead body shall they arise. Awake and sing, ye that dwell in dust for…the earth shall cast out the dead.

Daniel 12:2: And many of them that sleep in the dust of the earth shall awake, some to everlasting life, and some to shame and everlasting contempt.[7]

---

6   Moody, 1975.
7   The Holy Bible, King James Version.

CHAPTER 2

The Apostle Paul was a Christian persecutor until he had a vision and conversion on the road to Damascus. In the New Testament we find:

Acts 26:13: At midday, O king, I saw in the way a light from heaven, above the brightness of the sun, shining round about me and them which journeyed with me. And when we were all fallen to the earth, I heard a voice speaking unto me, and saying in the Hebrew tongue, "Saul, Saul, why persecutest thou me? It is hard for thee to kick against the pricks."

And I said, "Who art thou, Lord?" And he said, "I am Jesus, whom thou persecutest. But rise, and stand upon thy feet: for I have appeared unto thee for this purpose, to make thee a minister and a witness, both of these things in which I will appear unto thee...."

Whereupon, O King Agrippa, I was not disobedient unto the heavenly vision....

And as I thus spake for myself, Festus said with a loud voice, "Paul, thou art beside thyself; much learning does make thee mad."

But I said, "I am not mad, most noble Festus; but speak forth the words of truth and soberness."

Paul apparently had an encounter with a being of light. He was ridiculed when he tried to tell others of this experience, but this did not stop him from becoming a leading proponent of Christianity.

1 Corinthians 15:35–52: But some man will say, "How are the dead raised up? And with what body do they come?" Thou fool...(of) that which thou sowest, thou sowest not that body that shall be but bare grain....But God giveth it a body as it had pleased him, and to every seed his own body....There are also celestial bodies, and bodies terrestrial: but the glory of the celestial is one and the glory of the terrestrial is another....So also is the resurrection of the dead. It is sown in corruption, it is raised in in corruption: It is sown in dishonor; it is raised in glory: It is sown in weakness; it is raised in power: It is sown a natural body, it is raised a spiritual body. There is a natural body, and there is a spiritual body....Behold I show you a mystery: We shall not all sleep, but we shall all be changed. In a moment, in the twinkling of an eye, at the last trumpet: for the trumpet shall sound, and the dead shall be raised incorruptible.

Paul describes a "spiritual body," timeless, strong, and beautiful. Today many use the term *astral body* to refer to this source.

Plato recorded a resurrection episode when he described a dead soldier who, after leaving his body, came back to life and ascended to heaven. In the sixth century Pope Gregory the Great compiled resuscitation reports. (We will deal with other manuals of conscious dying in detail in Part III.)

EMANUEL SWEDENBORG (1688–1772)

Emanuel Swedenborg (1688–1772) was a natural scientist who devoted his later life to the study of metaphysics. (Swedenborg's earlier works will be treated in some detail in chapter 23.) He wrote of death:

Still man does not die, but is only separated from the corporeal part which was of use to him in the world....Man, when he dies, only passes from one world into another.

He also described his own NDE:

I was brought into a state of insensibility as to the bodily senses, thus almost into the state of the dying; yet the interior life with thought remaining entire, so that I perceived and retained in memory the things which occurred, and which occur to those who are resuscitated from the dead....Especially it was given to perceive...that there was a drawing and...pulling of...mind, thus of my spirit, from the body.

Swedenborg described Angels:

Those angels first inquired what my thought was, whether it was like the thought of those who die, which is usually about eternal life; and that they wished to keep my mind in that thought.

CHAPTER 2

…Whereas spirits converse with each other by a universal language….Every man, immediately after death, comes into this universal language …which is proper to his spirit….

The speech of an angel or a spirit with man is heard as sonorously as the speech of a man with a man; yet it is not heard by others who stand near, but by himself alone; the reason is, because the speech of an angel or spirit flows first into the man's thought….

He also noted that souls are not always aware that they have "died."

The first state of man after death is similar to his state in the world, because then in like manner he is in externals….Hence, he knows no otherwise than that he is still in the world ….Therefore, after they have wondered that they are in a body, and in every sense which they had in the world…they come into a desire of knowing what heaven is, and what hell is.

He relates the presence of spirit guides that help the soul:

The spirit of man recently departed from the world is…recognized by his friends, and by those whom he had known in the world…wherefore they are instructed by their friends concerning the state of eternal life….

The panoramic life review is also described:

The interior memory…is such that there are inscribed in it all the particular things…which man has at any time thought, spoken, and done…from his earliest infancy to extreme old age. Man has with him the memory of all these things when he comes into another life, and is successively brought into all recollection of them….All that he had spoken and done…are made manifest before the angels, in a light as clear as day…and…there is nothing so concealed in the world that it is not manifested after death…as if seen in effigy, when the spirit is viewed in the light of heaven.[8]

8 All Swedenborg quotations are taken from *Compendium of the Theological and Spiritual Writings of Emmanuel Swedenborg* (Boston: Crosby and Nichols, 1853), pp. 160–197, used with permission of the Swedenborg Foundation, West Chester, PA.

Albert Heim, a Swiss geologist and mountain climber, is considered to have been the first investigator to systematically gather data on near-death experiences. Working at the turn of the century, Heim interviewed some thirty skiers and climbers who had been involved in accidents resulting in paranormal experiences. Heim's subjects experienced such phenomena as detachment from their bodies and panoramic memory, or life review. These characteristics of near-death experiences have since become familiar to researchers in this area.

Since the 1960s, the work of Karlis Osis and Erlender Haraldsson and Raymond Moody, Elizabeth Kübler-Ross, and Kenneth Ring have given a firm foundation to NDE. These are but a few of the many dedicated researchers in this most unusual but rewarding discipline.

EXPLANATIONS FOR NEAR-DEATH EXPERIENCES

The classic psychoanalytical explanation for an NDE is that when a person's life is threatened, the ego activates a psychological defense mechanism creating the elements of the core experience. Others feel that the "happily ever after" stance toward death may represent a form of denial when what is really needed by the dying is a demonstration of real concern and real caring in their present experience.

This notion of a protective response provided as an escape for the ego when confronted by death, along with laboratory-induced after-life visions, fail to account for the overnight permanent personality changes that are observed. Included among these changes are healthier eating habits, improved self-images, and a greater zest for life. These people are not just saying they are different, they are acting empowered.

Cross-cultural studies of NDE have been conducted by the well-respected researchers Karlis Osis and Erlender Haraldsson. Their conclusions are that the evidence from NDEs are highly suggestive of life after death. Apparitions that are contrary to the expectations of the experiencer are especially significant. Children surprised at observing angels without wings and patients seeing people they assumed to be alive but were in fact dead support this hypothesis of life after death.

Neither cultural conditioning, nor medical or psychological theories can explain these.

Recent Gallup polls show that about sixty percent of Americans believe in hell. Yet no Euro-American NDE report indicates a judgment procedure. The life reviews always have love and comfort as the theme.

Another interesting fact about NDE is that there is such a similarity between the consciousness at death and that of life that the patient has difficulty in recognizing that they have shifted realities. This is supported by the Tibetan Buddhist belief that all of the bardos, including life, dying between lives, rebirth, hypnosis, and dreaming are basically identical in the dualistic structure and appearance.

My medical colleagues are quick to point out the biological effect of cerebral anoxia, or the effect of general anesthetics and narcotics used in a hospital. In order for this strictly neurophysiological explanation to carry weight, it would have to account for the entire core experience, but it most certainly does not. In addition, amnesia is a result of cerebral anoxia. NDE reports would not exist if cerebral anoxia was in effect. The presence and/or the "voice" often encountered during an NDE is most likely the Higher Self, not an extension of the personality.

SUMMARIZING NDE

- NDEs cannot be explained adequately on the basis of drugs, hallucinations, cultural conditioning, etc.

- Religion, race, and age are also unrelated to NDEs.

- Ninety-five percent of NDEs are positive and literally transform the personality of the recipient. Many patients do not want to return to the physical body because it is so positive.

- A Being of Light often conducts a panoramic life review of the patient during an NDE. Not only is every action observed, but the effects on others are noted. Telepathy is the mode of communication.

- The patient sometimes gets information about the future. Some of these precognitions have been documented.

- The overnight personality changes that occur, including greater zest for life, improved self-confidence, healthier eating habits, and increased compassion, simply cannot be explained by hallucinations or any other conjecture proposed by the skeptics critical of this experience.

- An NDE is one of the most powerful events a person can experience. It has redirected lives, created saints, inspired religions, and shaped history.

- NDEs are reported in thirty-five to forty percent of people who have a brush with death.

RELATING NDE TO CONSCIOUS DYING

An NDE is an example of unconscious dying. This is a prelude to many of the circumstances that a soul will encounter in conscious dying, with one great difference. That difference is related to the disorienting forces of the lower planes or karmic cycle, as I explained in chapter 1.

The advantage of maintaining contact with the Higher Self at the moment of death is that the soul can avoid the need to come back again to the earth plane, or any of the other lower planes. If these souls must return, their new life will be far more fulfilling and empowered than if they died unconsciously.

We can learn from NDEs what not to do. In addition, the phenomenon provides us with a glimpse of what death will be like. This should remove the fears commonly associated with this transition. It is this fear that disorients the soul upon death and creates many of the problems the transitee experiences when he or she dies unconsciously.

For those of you who are interested in learning more about NDEs, I recommend you contact:

The International Association for Near-Death Studies (IANDS)
P.O. Box 502
East Windsor, Connecticut 06028
Telephone: (203) 528-5144.

IANDS publishes a quarterly journal (*Journal of Near-Death Studies*) and a newsletter (*Vital Signs*). This organization is international, with members on every continent.

...the transition to what
we call death...
should be accompanied by
solemn joyousness

CHAPTER 3

The Cycle of Birth and Death

We have given up the awareness of our immortal soul and its spiritual powers by living only as physical bodies. The beauty and
healing effects that result from communion with spiritual beings, being
one with the universe, and the perception of the nonphysical dimensions of existence can be regained easily through conscious dying.

Our consciousness has become entirely secularized. We state that
death is inevitable and that we are mortal. Rollo May would call this
existential neurosis—to him this was the basic cause of all anxieties and
fears. Cleansing can and will remove this state of despair and insecurity. I refer to it as existential insecurity. This theme is also that of *The
Egyptian and Tibetan Book*[s] *of the Dead*, which should be called books
of the living (see Part III).

Cleansing is simply the ability to go through death consciously,
through birth consciously, between death and rebirth consciously, and
maintain the connection between the soul and Higher Self through
these various states, to help restore the integrity of the soul. This will,
in many cases, eliminate the need to reincarnate. If a future life on the
earth or other lower plane is indicated, it will be a far more spiritual

and fulfilling one. Thus the universe, as well as the individual soul, will benefit from conscious dying.

During cleansing, we will be able to recall our previous lives. We will become aware of our soul's true purpose, our karmic purpose. It will mean an end to the cycle of birth and death known as the karmic cycle. Christians call this salvation. The *Tibetan Book of the Dead* names this "clear light."[1] Buddhists call this "nirvana." Hindus use the term "moksha." I simply call it cleansing.

This book will illustrate that the only true source is your own consciousness. Your consciousness will be awakened by conscious dying. Learn, know, and die consciously (see chapter 10). Practice selfless service and love. Meditate, engage in self-hypnosis, yoga, or whatever will relax you naturally. There are no absolute truths, even what I just wrote.

If the purpose of being born into a physical body is to learn how not to be born again, not being born again is achieved by learning how not to become unconscious before, during, and after the moment of dying. This concept has been presented many times before in history. It appears in *Per em ru* (*Egyptian Book of the Dead*), Dante's *Divine Comedy*, The Tenth Book of Plato's *The Republic*, the Sixth Book of Virgil's *Aeneid*, the *Garuda Purana* of India, the Orphic manual called *The Descent Into Hades,* Swedenborg's *De Coelo et de Infero* and *The Seven Sermons of the Dead* by Basilides. I will further develop this history in Part III.

This is not meant to be a treatise, but merely a guidebook. Its main purpose is to help the reader learn to die consciously and to do this on a daily basis. This is the very essence of enlightenment and immortality.

This book is not just a guidebook to conscious dying. It will train you to maintain the integrity and continuity of consciousness (the connection between the soul and the Higher Self) after dying, through the intermediate state between death and rebirth, and through the process of being reborn, including both the inter-uterine phase as well as the birth phase of rebirth.

---

1 Evans-Wentz, 1960.

This allows us to learn to again live as a nonphysical being. By regaining this lost awareness of our inherent immortality, our consciousness will finally be liberated from its limitations. Cleansing will prevent a break in the continuity and integrity of our consciousness through death, bardo, and rebirth (if necessary). This spiritual realization and actualization is required if we are going to eliminate the cycle of birth and death.

As Buddha recalled all of his past lives when he attained Nirvana under the Bodhi tree, so will you access your Akashic record and learning about yours. Our immortality has not been lost, merely our awareness of it. We tend to exhibit a form of spiritual amnesia about our true nature and origin.

Conscious dying is intended for use by all beings, irrespective of their religious inclinations or beliefs. In fact, it may be used even by those who choose not to have, or not to belong to, any religion or religious group at all. After all, a person can be religious without having a religion, or have a religion without being religious.

When we are in our spiritual (astral) body we are able to see without using physical eyes; able to hear without using ears; and able to think and feel without physical brain and endocrine glands. Buddha Gautama spoke of the Buddha-potential in everyone. He stated that the main difference between a Buddha and a non-Buddha is that a Buddha knows he is a Buddha and behaves like one, whereas a non-Buddha does not know he is a Buddha and therefore does not behave like one.

Instead, we identify ourselves with the body as well as with everything that happens to the body—birth, death, and all the happenings between, such as getting sick, getting old, suffering, and, of course, all the forms of existential neurosis and phobias, such as fear of pain, fear of sickness, fear of losing, fear of dying, and even fear of fear itself.

We also identify ourselves with our minds and all their insecurities and prejudices; and we identify ourselves with our emotions, with all our struggles and sufferings. We have become victims of our thoughts and our passions. As such we remain trapped in the cycle of birth and death, connected by the psychological and physiological energies making up the chain of causes and effects that result in our physical being.

Buddhists refer to this chain of sequential causes as Nidanas. There are twelve of these Nidanas that are reportedly responsible for the karmic cycle. By dying and being reborn unconsciously humanity has assumed:

- The inability to manage and control one's life.

- Slavery to external circumstances, birth without permission, and death without consent.

- The lack of awareness of the universe or God.

- The illusion of identification with the ego.

- The illusion of identification with the physical body.

- The illusion of identification with the mind-emotion process.

These Nidanas are the specific forces that we use to create and recreate ourselves, both physically and nonphysically. We can use these energies by dying consciously to direct our lives to greater wisdom, freedom, and joy. We can utilize the natural resources we possess as liberating forces to free us of karma. By dying unconsciously, we then become enslaved to these energies and are bound to the cycle of birth and death.

The Nidanas act in sequence, one force bringing about the next in a chain reaction. Ignorance is the most basic Nidana. Our lack of knowledge of our true nature as spiritual beings (souls) leads us astray. We then identify only with our physical body. By assuming that the mind is merely a by-product of the brain we only add to our ignorance.

Each Nidana acts in sequence as follows: energies are expressed through conditioned senses (*salayatana*); these conditioned senses can make possible only conditioned contact with what is (*phasssa*); this conditioned contact can produce only conditioned feelings (*vedana*); these conditioned feelings can awaken only conditioned cravings or desires (*tanha*); these conditioned cravings can create only conditioned attachments (*upadana*); these conditioned attachments can lead only to conditioned becoming (*bhava*) and conditioned birth (*jati*); and this conditioned birth naturally would involve again the chain-suffering of aging (*jara*), dying (*mara*), grieving (*soka*), sorrowing (*parideva*), suffering (*dukkha*), lamenting (*domanassa*), and despairing (*upayasa*).

When we liberate ourselves from this ignorance, as in conscious dying, we enter a wheel of empowerment. *The Sermon on the Mount* from the *Gospel of Saint Matthew* is probably the most complete description of the Christian Path of Perfection.

In Hinduism there is the *Nivritti Marga*, the Path of Liberation from the *vrittis* or conditioning activities of the mind (*chitta*). The methods and techniques of liberation are described in the *Ashtanga Yoga*, or the Eight Limbs of Yoga given in the *Yogasutras* of Patanjali.

In Buddhism the Path of Liberation is called *Ashtanga Arya Marga*, the Noble Eightfold Path. It describes the eight steps by which one is able to get out of the cycle of birth and death.

In order to fully understand and appreciate just what the cycle of birth and death is, we must deal with the plane concept. There are theories that state the presence of seven lower planes. My clinical experience since 1974 in conducting over 33,000 past life regressions and future life progressions on well over 11,000 individual patients has led to the following deductions about the karmic cycle.

Our karmic cycle, according to the plane concept, is worked out on five lower planes. Our soul is characterized by a level of awareness or vibrational rate. You must raise the quality of your vibrational rate to ascend to a higher plane. Each successive plane requires a higher vibrational rate. The entity will seek the plane that best fits its level.

THE LOWER FIVE PLANES

1. The *earth plane* or *physical plane*. This is the plane that we function in now. The body is most material or physical at this level. The greatest amount of karma can be erased or added on at this level. This is by far the most difficult level.

2. The *astral plane*. The body is less material here. This is where the subconscious, or soul, goes immediately following death or crossing over. Ghosts are examples of astral bodies.

3. The *causal plane*. The body is even less material at this level. The akashic records are kept here. This is where a medium projects him or herself when he or she reads your past or future.

4. The *mental plane*. This is the plane of pure intellect.

5. The *etheric plane*. The body is least material at this level. On this plane, truth and beauty are the ultimate values.

It is the thoughts and actions of the soul that determine the amount of time spent on these lower planes. Each of these planes is noted for providing an environment to learn certain spiritual lessons. For example, truth is associated with the etheric plane, while intellectual tasks are deferred to the mental plane. The earth plane represents the plane of greatest elimination or addition to our karmic debts.

Akashic Records

The Akashic records are a type of chart of all of your past, present, and future lifetimes. They are reportedly kept on the causal plane. These records are what psychics and channelers access when they initiate a reading. We have the capacity to access these records on any plane, but it is easiest to obtain this data on the soul plane. These records accurately reflect our soul's growth and what we have yet to learn.

THE SOUL PLANE

This plane (plane 6) is an intermediary or "demilitarized zone" between the lower planes and higher planes. This is where the Higher Self spends most of its time, and it is here that a soul chooses its next lifetime. The white light, as often described by near-death experiencers, is actually the Higher Self, which escorts the soul to the soul plane. Masters and Guides and departed loved ones may also be in attendance at this location. Telepathy is the mode of communication and there are no secrets. Any entity now can literally read your mind, so truth in its pure form is evident.

You will be shown fragments of your most recent incarnation here, along with several other of your past lives and future life options. The Masters and Guides and your Higher Self will often advise, but it is always your choice as to your next life. The soul always has free will. Naturally, you would probably not have to reincarnate if you success-fully practiced conscious dying when you were in the physical body. If you must reincarnate on the lower planes, remember life on these other planes isn't very different from that on the earth plane. People get mar-ried, have children, divorce, love, hate, etc. on all of the lower planes.

	God or Nameless	*Plane 13*
		Plane 12
Seven		Plane 11
Higher		Plane 10
Planes		Plane 9
		Plane 8
		Plane 7
	Soul Plane	*Plane 6*
Karmic	Etheric	Plane 5
Cycle —	Mental	Plane 4
Five	Causal	Plane 3—*Akashic Records*
Lower	Astral	Plane 2
Planes	Earth	Plane 1—*You Are Here*

Figure 2
The Progression of the 13 Planes

THE SEVEN HIGHER PLANES

You may choose any of the lower five planes to work out your karma, but as long as you have a karmic cycle you cannot enter the seven high-er planes—your vibrational rate would be too low to permit it.

These seven higher planes reach their apex with the God or name-less plane (Number 13). The essence—our true nature—resides on the God plane. It is our SOURCE, the ONE, ALL THAT IS, and many other descriptive names—this is the heaven or nirvana we have come to know by our religious training.

The quality of your spiritual growth as manifested by your soul's frequency vibrational rate determines which plane you are able to enter. Your thoughts and actions control this quality. If your vibrational rate qualifies you for the tenth plane, then you cannot enter any high-er plane until this rate is increased appropriately.

This concept does not include a Hell. Hell is simply the negative lives you live on the earth plane. There is, however, a heaven or nir-vana. It is part of your empowerment to control your thoughts and actions so that you may once again join with God.

The plane concept can best be illustrated by the diagram on the previous page (Fig. 2). From this diagram of the cycle of birth and death, you can see that it is no picnic. The most desirable solution is to perfect the soul as quickly as possible and ascend into the higher planes. Another option is to remain on as a Master or Guide and assist other souls in their ascension. The fastest route to this perfect state is conscious dying.

The energies of the universe, both physical and nonphysical, are at our disposal. We either use them correctly, or misuse and abuse them. Sometimes we do not use them at all because we do not know how.

To some extent we have learned how to use physical energies. We have developed sciences and technologies of physical energy by which we have created some conveniences and comforts in our physical lives. We have also misused and abused these energies, resulting in the pol-lution of our environment, the poisoning of our bloodstream, and the ever-present threat of nuclear destruction.

Our ignorance is manifested in the energy of thought. We deal with it only as an electro-chemical reaction in the brain cells. The energy of consciousness is dealt with in a similar way. As far as the energy of love is concerned, we mistakenly regard it as merely physical sexual energy.

Western science totally rejects the energy of the spirit, called kundalini in the East. According to this unenlightened and limited point of view, emotional energy is an expression mainly of glandular secretions; mental energy is a manifestation of brain action; and spiritual energy does not exist at all, despite evidence to the contrary in many cases in which consciousness, thought, and reason persist in spite of the sense of cerebral activity (EEG).

These nonphysical energies operate in our lives, whether we accept that they exist or not, whether we are conscious of them or not. Non-acceptance of the fact of gravitation and non-awareness of its energy transformation do not exempt or exclude us from its universal effect upon all material bodies.

By using the connection of our subconscious mind (soul) to our superconscious mind (Higher Self) we can transform the Nidanas into liberating forces, freeing us from the karmic cycle. We can then create our own freedom and joy.

Different religions and different teachers have chosen one or two, or any combination of these twelve liberating forces, and emphasized their choices as the way to liberation.

Buddhism has stressed Right Meditation as the way to *Nirvana*, otherwise called *Satipatthana* Meditation, or Right Mindfulness.

Christianity, exemplified by St. Paul, emphasizes the "Awakening of Love" as the liberating process. Christ declared that Love of God and Love of Fellow-Beings constitute the greatest commandment. St. Paul, in the thirteenth chapter of his First Epistle to the Corinthians, declared in no uncertain terms that love is the way to perfection, of meeting God face to face, and of knowing, even as God knows.

Transpersonal psychology emphasizes the use of altered states of consciousness as a path to higher consciousness and the further ranges of human life. Liberation from the cycle of birth and death is a liberation of consciousness from its man-made limitations, mostly resulting from unconscious death and rebirth.

Easterners emphasize the integrity of the whole rather than the difference between component parts. To them unity underlies what may appear to be contradictory phenomena. They promote the concept that such apparent contrasts are merely illusory aspects of an undivided reality.

REINCARNATION

The *I Ching* or *Book of Changes* presents a world that is constantly being transformed. Life and death are simply manifestations of a constantly changing reality. Death and life are viewed as complementary aspects of an underlying process, not as mutually exclusive opposites.

Reincarnation is the best example of Eastern thought along this line. Through death, the soul is renewed by a succeeding lifetime in another body. This concept of transmigration illustrates the continuing process of life and death. As Lao Tse, the Chinese philosopher, stated, "Birth is not a beginning and death is not an end."

According to the Hindus, individual souls transmigrate through a succession of bodies. This passing through, or samsara, is linked by karma. Karma is the moral law of cause and effect. The individual's present state of being is determined by the soul's past thoughts and deeds. These, in turn, influence future states. This constantly changing flow of moment-to-moment experience leading to successive rounds of deaths and rebirths (the cycle of birth and death) is controlled by karma. At the center of life is a hidden self, or *Atman*, which is the soul.

Christianity, in its orthodox form, rejects the concept of reincarnation and acknowledges only one universe. This is the first and last universe, and we have two lives, one here in the physical body and one hereafter in the body of the Resurrection.

Other Eastern religions, such as Buddhism, Islam, and Brahmanism, accept the doctrine of reincarnation. These Easterners feel that a Heaven does exist, but not that a resurrected body ascends to it. Rather it is consciousness (the soul) that voyages.

All of these faiths allude to a continuation of the soul in some afterlife. Death is only a doorway to another form of life than the one that is ending.

New karma is not created in the afterlife. The bardo (in-between life) experience is merely the result of the actions and thoughts of the physical life. Hinduism, Christianity, and Buddhism, for example, all agree that a human's destiny is decided on earth.

There is no breach of consciousness, but a continuity of transformation. Death-Consciousness is the starting point. Karma generates a fully formed desire or mental action. This action is followed by bardo experiences and an eventual rebirth. The main point here is to effect a higher quality (more spiritual) new life, until perfection of the soul is achieved.

Death and the Fate of the Soul

The last thought and utterance at the moment of death, according to Hindus and Buddhists, determines the quality of the soul's next life. By "rightly directing" this thought process of a dying person, conscious dying will result. It is preferable if the dying person has had a lifetime of preparation for this climactic moment. Indian sages also teach that a friend, relative, or guru well versed in conscious dying techniques may assist the voyager.

Eastern philosophy clearly states that our present thinking determines our future status. Along the same line, our past thinking has significantly influenced our present status.

Responding to Death

The transition to what we call death can and should be accompanied by solemn joyousness—a peaceful transition. In India, the term *Samadhi* is used to describe this state. By practicing conscious dying, the fear of death will be overcome and the soul will be truly empowered. One soul may assist another in this transition. The Moslem's *Fatiha*, the *Pretashraddha* of Hinduism, and the Requiem Mass in Catholicism are modern examples of attempts at conscious dying.

The dying should face death not only calmly and clear-mindedly and heroically, but with an intellect rightly trained and rightly directed, mentally transcending bodily suffering and infirmities, as they would be able to do had they practiced efficiently during their active lifetime the art of conscious dying. In the West where this technique is little known and rarely practiced, there is, contrastingly, a common unwillingness to die.

With the aid of psychology, the rationalizing mind of the West has pushed forward into what one might call metaphysical neuroticism, and has there been brought to an inevitable standstill by the uncritical assumption that everything psychological is subjective and personal. Even so, this advance has been a great gain, inasmuch as it has enabled us to take one more step behind our conscious lives.

The ultimate effect of
aging is, of course,
death.

CHAPTER 4

Current Attitudes Toward Dying

The human concern for the dead predates written history. Over
50,000 years ago Neanderthals buried ornamented shells, stone
tools, and food with their dead. This implied a belief that the recently departed would have some need for these items during the soul's
transition. In some grave sites the corpse was placed in a fetal position and stained with red ocher, further suggesting a belief in rebirth.

Among prehistoric cultures death appeared to be viewed as a transition from the world of the living to that of the dead. Death was not
viewed as an extinction. The ancient Egyptians carried on this tradition.

During the Middle Ages, every Christian church and cathedral had
a bell tower. When someone died a fee was paid for the ringing of the
"soul" bell. This served as a form of public notification that someone
had died. Who can forget John Dunne's immortal line, "for whom the
bell tolls," signifying this event. Bells were also used in the Orient to
help counsel a spirit away from the dead body. These societies also felt
the sound of the bell would drive away "evil spirits" from the recently
departed. If they had practiced conscious dying techniques, this could
have been avoided.

The investigation of death plagues one with queries that are at the very center of human experience. This becomes a personal and experiential journey of discovery, stressing the values of listening, compassion, and tolerance of the views of others. I can think of no other experience with greater impact on our life. However, Americans deal with death from the position of denial.

A hundred years ago the phenomenon of death was handled quite differently than it is today. Death usually occurred in the home, with family members present. Certain rituals were practiced and a coffin was built for the body, which was then placed in the parlor of the home. The family's mourning was shared by relatives (including children), friends, and other members of the community. The coffin was open so that callers could view the body, and prayers might be offered. A funeral service was held, and the body was then taken to the gravesite. Everyone learned about death firsthand.

Today things are done quite differently. Family and friends are merely observers, instead of active participants. We pay others to perform the services of preparing the dead for burial. Modern mortuaries sell elaborate caskets and cosmetic restoration of the corpse diminishes the appearance of death. During the funeral the casket is closed and often not even in view of the family. Death is tastefully disguised. This is denial.

The average life expectancy in the United States has risen from forty-seven at the turn of the century to over seventy-five today. Over half of the reported deaths one hundred years ago involved people fifteen years of age and younger. Today that figure is only about five percent.

The death rate in America was about seventeen per 1,000 in 1900. This has declined to approximately 8.7 deaths per 1,000. This lower rate makes it easier to deny death, especially since the very young are surviving at much higher levels than ever in our history.

A hundred years ago the typical transition was sudden—often due to acute infectious diseases such as diphtheria, septicemia, typhoid, and tuberculosis. Those infections accounted for about forty percent of all deaths in the United States. Today only four percent of deaths result from these infections. Death is usually a slow, progressive process resulting from heart disease or cancer.

Since about eighty percent of us die in an institution, death is separated from our day-to-day life. A patient dying of a terminal illness often is not told of his or her impending death. Many relatives are informed of the death of a family member by a telephone call. No longer is there firsthand experience of the transition of a loved one. Like sex, death is a secret to be whispered out of hearing range. Our entire society is conditioned to deny death and anything associated with it.

Sympathy cards are an example of society's denial of death. In less than three percent of the cards I have read was the word "death" mentioned. The terms "death," "died," and "killed" are carefully avoided when writing letters. We like to use euphemisms such as "passed on," "gone to heaven," "expired," "given up the ghost," "departed," "perished," "resting in peace," or "bought the farm."

Our society thinks nothing of spending billions of dollars annually on cosmetics, hair dyes, face lifts, or diets, but we simply cannot deal with aging. Gray hair, lowered energy, weight gain, and other physical effects of aging are covered up or cosmetically doctored so we don't have to deal with them. The ultimate effect of aging is, of course, death.

We live in a society based on material gain, and neither aging nor death add to our net worth, so why acknowledge it? I work with many patients individually who are scared to death of death. Conscious dying does solve these problems. Conscious dying allows us to rise above insecurities and superficialities.

Few people can recognize and accept the concept that the body is just a temporary vehicle for the soul. They cling so hard to their physical structure that they are afraid to face reality. The lack of a belief in the immortality of the soul is, in my experience, the main reason for society's greatest fear, the fear of death.

In our highly technological society we tend to view the death of the young as tragic. Native Americans have a much different outlook. They look upon life in a circular fashion, with puberty being the time when the circle is complete. From that time on the wholeness of one's life is established, and whenever death occurs one dies in wholeness. It is the fullness with which one enters each complete moment that determines wholeness; wholeness is thus not related to the length of life but to its quality.

Most depression and anxiety that I have observed in the over 11,000 individual patients I have seen in my office emanates from their futile attempt to re-create the pleasures of the past and to prevent the pains of unfulfilled yearnings from happening in the future. This philosophy simply cannot work. Evidence of psychosomatic illness originating from repressed emotions aside, we just cannot control basic events in our lives—or can we?

Conscious dying empowers us. It affords us the opportunity to custom design our future and to control events within a certain range. For people who don't die consciously (which is practically everyone on this planet) panic ensues when reality fails to conform with their image of how things are. They hide. They stay in their homes and hope that if they deny death and its discomfort long and hard enough, just maybe it will go away.

This "I-ness" or "me-ness" is one thing most of us seem unwilling to lose. In death we fear that we will lose our "I." The more we attempt to protect ourselves, the less we experience anything else. The loss will be that of our ability to experience a deeper perception and understanding of what death is and the reality of a peaceful transition. The more we posture and postpone life, the more we fear death.

Again I refer to the Native American culture. They use a death chant to cultivate an openness to death. Certain rites of passage are practiced, such as going into the wilderness alone for many days of prayer and fasting. There they are open to receive a guiding message from a spirit to counsel them in their life, a component of attaining wholeness. This spirit is often the source of their individual death chant.

The death chant is used in times of great stress or peril. A confrontation with a dangerous animal or the threat of death from an illness would bring the death chant to consciousness, resulting in a desensitization and familiarity with death. When the time comes to actually use this chant at the moment of death, a conscious dying ensues.

Being open to whatever happens is a major component to conscious dying. If you exclude only death from your "everything is okay" list, eventually you will add other items to this compilation. Soon nothing is okay and everything is to be feared. Some call that civilization. It is this limiting of what is acceptable that isolates us and causes us to abandon the good along with the bad.

Television offers us another example of society's fixation with death. The media image of death is frequently characterized by violence. It presents a depersonalized image of death so that its very concept is blurred. This is one way to deny the end result.

My review of a typical week of program listings in *TV Guide* showed about one-third of the shows featured death or dying. I was not counting newscasts, nature programs, cartoons, religions programming, sports, or soap operas. Seldom do these depictions add to our knowledge of the reality of death. When you next see a television show or featured film, watch closely when death is portrayed.

The death scene will most likely be violent. If the actor dies slowly he or she will no doubt pass away in perfect harmony to the music. The less the viewer can identify with this depiction of death, the more the denial of their own fate. "What you don't know won't hurt you" may sound good to some people, but it is denial.

The print media presents death in a more realistic and therapeutic fashion. Books such as Elizabeth Kübler-Ross' *On Death and Dying*[1] focus on the feelings and needs of the dying patient. It was a truly radical notion in 1969, when this book first appeared, that health care professionals and the patient's family could learn something from a dying human being.

Glaser and Strauss' book *Awareness of Dying*[2] showed that both medical professionals and the public were hesitant to discuss the process of dying and tried to avoid telling a patient that he or she was dying.

---

1 Elizabeth Kübler Ross, *On Death and Dying* (New York: Macmillan, 1969).
2 Barney G. Glaser and Anselm L. Strauss, *Awareness of Dying* (Hawthorne, NY: Aldine de Gruyter, 1969).

Hospice organizations give hope in that they illustrate how the previous contrary attitudes toward dying can be successfully adapted in a modern social setting. Among the Amish death is considered part of the natural rhythm of life. They practice such rituals as the continued presence of the family, keeping a normal lifestyle during this time, open communication about the process of dying and its impact on the family, empowering the dying person, and continued support of the bereaved.

The best hope we have for society in dealing with death is the theme of this book: conscious dying. Life-threatening experiences that do not involve NDEs actually decrease the fear of death. Researcher Russell Noyes Jr. of the University of Iowa College of Medicine noted these remarks made by survivors:[3]

> Auto-accident victims: "I had never thought I would give up but when I realized I could die and there was still no fear....The fear of dying left me." "I have no fear, almost welcoming...that there are better and more beautiful experiences after this life."

> Survivor of carbon monoxide poisoning: "If I am not afraid to die, neither am I afraid to live—that is, to approach people, be friendly and so forth. It has enabled me to try anything I have...."

> Sixteen-year-old survivor of gunshot wound: "I am grateful to be alive, but I think it is because God wanted me to live."

Noyes noted that the attitude changes closely resembled those seen following NDEs. He also noted that shamanic rituals bring about a similar healing result. The lesson here seems to be that it takes a crisis to bring us to our senses about death. I say let's forget the need for a crisis and practice conscious dying daily.

---

3   Russell Noyes Jr. *Brain/Mind Bulletin*, May 3, 1976, 1, 12f.

...there is no death
...there is only
a shift
in awareness

CHAPTER 5

The Higher Self

The superconscious mind is also referred to as the Higher Self. This is literally the perfect part of our soul's energy. It is a remnant of the God energy from which we all derive. The Higher Self's memory is perfect and objective. It has access to our akashic records and can communicate with our subconscious mind at any time, day or night.

According to theosophical theory (see chapter 24), the Higher Self consists of three components: *Atma, Manas*, and *Buddhi*. The subconscious mind or soul is often named the lower self and manifests itself into the astral plane of Kamaloka if the death is an unconscious one. The specific carriers of karma are known as *Skandhas*. There are four factors predominant in choosing a new life:

- Free will.

- Karmic ties with friends and family members.

- The learning potential of the new life.

- Special assignments that have been previously accepted.

The four or seven Lords of Karma, known as Lipika, direct the karmic cycle. They reportedly have a direct incentive to keep this system going, for without unevolved souls they would have nothing to do and no one to control.

There are four components of karmic lessons:

- Artha or material advancement. Avarice is the biggest problem here.

- Moksha, or deliverance from physical limitations and from reincarnation itself.

- Karma, or lust. Anger is the weakness of this type.

- . Dharma, or moral and religious virtue and integrity.

Scientists actually do try to explain the Higher Self or superconscious mind. What Easterners refer to as pure light, clear light, or pure consciousness, quantum physicists describe as simply consciousness. Evan Harris Walker was the first quantum physicist to develop a mathematical model of this phenomenon. His model postulated that the basic unit of consciousness is the quantum itself.

According to the new physics, all reality is interconnected at the deepest levels. Observations performed on one object can affect the data readings taken on another. They may not be in physical contact at all—they may even be light-years apart—but in the most profound, universal sense, they are never out of contact with each other. It is the Higher Self that bridges these gaps. Pure consciousness is beyond space-time; a duality exists. We certainly cannot understand fully the nature of the Higher Self, yet neither can we ignore its presence. A scientific impasse has resulted.

ANGELS

The Higher Self has often been confused and mislabeled as an angelic encounter. I do not doubt that such Higher Self exposures can be construed by the recipient, usually a soul in time of great stress, as a visit by their Guardian Angel. The one objection I have to this labeling is the theological definition and classification of angels.

Theologians clearly declare that angels are totally separate from human souls. These messengers of God were never human and no human can ever become an angel. This divergent evolution is contrary to all of the evidence I have accumulated from the superconscious mind taps conducted on the many thousands of patients I have seen since 1974. I have purposely eliminated many of the negative portrayals of angels by various religions and present the New Age version of these entities.

There are certain components to this theological concept:

- Angels exist in a different universe than humans.

- They enter our world through a type of doorway to make themselves known to us.

- They have consciousness, will, and purpose.

- Angels are always messengers, protectors, and guardians.

- They are universal, being a component of all religions.

- Angels do not disturb our free will. We can ignore them if we want to.

- The only creed an angel has is love.

- They can be anywhere they want in an instant.

- An angel is going to appear to us in whatever way it believes is best suited for drawing our attention; such appearances are calculated to maximize our response to their message, spurring us to action.

- Angels communicate by telepathy.

Four factors determine whether we will have a face-to-face contact with our angels. Such contact must be part of God's plan. We must truly understand what angels are and do, as well as what they will not or cannot do. Our motives for wanting such an encounter must be pure, and we must be prepared for an encounter.

Angels will use whatever medium is most likely to attract our attention. Very often they will utilize our dreams to help us.

There are some key characteristics of angelic experiences. Their message leaves us confident, never anxious, and they don't try to force us to do anything. Angels don't leave us confused. Their messages are designed to give us freedom to choose. An angelic encounter leaves us changed for the better in some way. Does this not sound like the mechanism and action of the Higher Self?

To invite an encounter with an angel through hypnosis is one of the most beautiful experiences you will ever have. The following script may be used to initiate such an experience:

ANGEL ENCOUNTERS SCRIPT

Now listen carefully. I want you to imagine a bright white light coming down from above and entering the top of your head, filling your entire body. See it, feel it, and it becomes reality. Now imagine an aura of pure white light emanating from your heart region, again surrounding your entire body, protecting you. See it, feel it, and it becomes reality. Now only angels and highly evolved loving entities who mean you well will be able to influence you during this or any other hypnotic session. You are totally protected by this aura of pure white light.

In a few moments, I am going to count from 1 to 20. As I do so, you will feel yourself rising up to the superconscious mind level, where you will be able to receive information from your angel protectors. Number 1 rising up. 2, 3, 4, rising higher. 5, 6, 7, letting information flow. 8, 9, 10, you are halfway there. 11, 12, 13, feel yourself rising even higher. 14, 15, 16, almost there. 17, 18, 19, number 20, you are there. Take a moment and orient yourself to the superconscious mind level.

PLAY NEW AGE MUSIC FOR 1 MINUTE

You may contact any of your angels from this level. You may explore your relationship with any person. Remember, your superconscious mind level is all-knowledgeable and has access to your akashic records. Let your Higher Self send out the appropriate energy to attract one of your angels.

Now slowly and carefully state your desire for information or an experience, and let this superconscious mind level work for you. Feel the healing energy and love coming from your Guardian Angel.

PLAY NEW AGE MUSIC FOR 8 MINUTES

You have done very well. Now I want you to further open up the channels of communication by removing any obstacles and allowing yourself to receive information and experiences that will directly apply to and help better your present lifetime. Allow yourself to receive more advanced and more specific information from your Higher Self and angels to raise your frequency and improve your karmic subcycle. Do this now.

PLAY NEW AGE MUSIC FOR 8 MINUTES

All right now. Sleep now and rest. You did very well. Listen very carefully. I'm going to count forward now from 1 to 5. When I reach the count of 5 you will be back in the present; you will be able to remember everything you experienced and re-experienced. You'll feel very relaxed, refreshed, and you'll be able to do whatever you have planned for the rest of the day or evening. You'll feel very positive about what you've just experienced and very motivated about your confidence and ability to play this tape again to experience your angels. All right now. 1, very, very deep, 2, you're getting a little bit lighter, 3, you're getting much much lighter, 4, very, very light, 5, awaken. Wide awake and refreshed.

In 1977, when I developed the field of progression hypnotherapy, the superconscious mind tap became the main technique in my practice. A superconscious mind tap is simply training the subconscious mind (soul) to communicate with the superconscious mind (Higher Self).

The superconscious mind tap is particularly valuable in our discussion because it trains the patient to raise the quality of their own subconscious mind's frequency vibrational rate. It also promotes contact and communication with lost loved ones, and overviews past and future lives with that loved one. The mind tap also facilitates finding out exactly why the loved one chose that time and method of dying (crossing into spirit), and trains the patient in the art of conscious dying.

A very therapeutic and efficient use of the superconscious mind tap and resultant communication with our Higher Self is that of directing our current subconscious mind. By contacting and accessing the Higher Self patients can review their karmic purpose, receiving summaries of their past and future lives. This is far less time-consuming than a step-by-step past life regression and future life progression. In my Los Angeles practice, I speed up this process by the use of conditioning self-hypnosis cassettes.

The script presented here may be used as the basis of your own tape. If you do not choose to make a tape, learn the high points of this script, but do not worry about memorizing it word for word. Your own Higher Self will assist you in attaining this all-important contact with the perfect component of your soul.

SUPERCONSCIOUS MIND SCRIPT

Now listen very carefully. I want you to imagine a bright white light coming down from above and entering the top of your head, filling your entire body. See it, feel it, and it becomes reality. Now imagine an aura of pure white light emanating from your heart region. Again surrounding your entire body. Protecting you. See it, feel it, and it becomes reality. Now only your Masters and Guides and highly evolved loving entities who mean you well will be able to influence you during this or any other hypnotic session. You are totally protected by this aura of pure white light.

In a few moments I am going to count from 1 to 20. As I do so you will feel yourself rising up to the superconscious mind level where you will be able to receive information from your Masters and Guides. You will also be able to overview all of your past, present, and future lives. Number 1 rising up. 2,

3, 4, rising higher. 5, 6, 7, letting information flow. 8, 9, 10, you are halfway there. 11, 12, 13, feel yourself rising even higher. 14, 15, 16, almost there. 17, 18, 19, number 20, you are there. Take a moment and orient yourself to the superconscious mind level.

PLAY NEW AGE MUSIC FOR 1 MINUTE

You may now ask yourself any question about any past, present, or future life issue. Or, you may contact any of your Guides or departed loved ones from this level. You may explore your relationship with any person. Remember, your superconscious mind level is all knowledgeable and has access to your akashic records.

Now slowly and carefully state your desire for information or an experience, and let this superconscious mind level work for you.

PLAY NEW AGE MUSIC FOR 8 MINUTES

You have done very well. Now I want you to further open up the channels of communication by removing any obstacles and allowing yourself to receive information and experiences that will directly apply to and help better your present lifetime. Allow yourself to receive more advanced and more specific information from your Higher Self and Masters and Guides to raise your frequency and improve your karmic sub-cycle. Do this now.

PLAY NEW AGE MUSIC FOR 8 MINUTES

All right now. Sleep now and rest. You did very very well. Listen very carefully. I'm going to count forward now from 1 to 5. When I reach the count of 5 you will be back in the present, you will be able to remember everything you experienced and re-experienced, you'll feel very relaxed, refreshed, you'll be able to do whatever you have planned for the rest of the day or evening. You'll feel very positive about what you've just experienced and very motivated about your confidence and ability to play this tape again to experience the superconscious mind level. All right now. 1, very, very deep, 2, you're getting a little bit lighter, 3, you're getting much much lighter, 4, very, very light, 5, awaken. Wide awake and refreshed.

Jerry Springer's Experience

An excellent example of this technique was provided by the syndicated television talk show host, Jerry Springer. I conducted a Higher Self communication with him that was taped in December 1993. Jerry is a former city councilman and two-term mayor of Cincinnati. He projects himself as a responsible citizen with a strong interest in providing a service for the public.

As a knight in England during the 1600s, Jerry was severely wounded in a battle defending the honor of a noblewoman. He could no longer function as a knight, so the woman he saved employed him as a butler. This woman reincarnated as Jerry's current-life daughter.

In the latter part of the next century, Jerry will be a rancher/farmer named Bobby who lives and works in Montana. He is married and has four children. Bobby is involved with a government project designed to raise crops on our moon. He will be killed at the age of sixty when his craft crashes during a return trip to Earth.

Jerry's Higher Self experience led to much information about his compassion for the needs of society. Two interesting facts surfaced from this future-life progression. First, Jerry's future-life wife is a girl he knew in high school named Robin. Second, he stated on his show that to this day he is afraid to dive into a pool, a phobia that has led to much embarrassment during past vacations. The progression pointed out a connection with his fear of water that apparently originates in a future life.

This next case illustrates how the Higher Self can communicate with us in a past life to facilitate the solution to the situation that seems hopeless. In a primitive past life in the Amazon jungle, my patient is a young male named Moke. The chief of his tribe, Sagu, was a very large and evil man. Moke challenged Sagu to fight to the death so that he could rid the tribe of this thug. Sagu was a very poor leader who only cared about fulfilling his selfish and ruthless cravings, often at the expense of the tribe's safety.

The problem was that Sagu was a much bigger man than Moke and the chief was the most skillful warrior in the tribe. This challenge seemed to forbode almost certain death for Moke.

Moke accessed his Higher Self and obtained the instructions for a plan to defeat Sagu. Moke went into the jungle and cleared some land to construct a trap for Sagu. He dug a deep ditch and placed very sharp wooden stakes at the bottom, then covered up the ditch.

The young chief-to-be then met secretly with a few of his close friends and they prepared a very special surprise for their chief. On the day of the challenge, Moke selected long poles as the weapons for the battle, as was the custom.

As the contest was about to begin Moke relocated this event to the carefully prepared spot in the jungle where the trap was constructed. Sagu was positioned in front of the camouflaged ditch. Suddenly a loud roar was heard behind Sagu. Moke stood there with his eyes wide open and a look of terror on his face. Some of the other tribesmen also stared at "something." As Sagu turned to face the cause of this horror, Moke picked up his pole and lunged forward. Sagu fell back a few steps and the grass opened up and all that was heard was a horrible scream.

Moke had constructed some kind of horn that when used in a certain way made an animal sound that was quite loud. One of the men in the tribe made this sound when Moke gave him a certain signal.

That momentary distraction as Sagu turned around was all that Moke needed to execute his plan. When Sagu fell into the pit he was instantly killed by the wooden stakes. Moke became chief and the tribe was rid of this cruel and sadistic leader.

In my first book, *Past Lives—Future Lives*,[1] I described a future lifetime of a woman who worked as an anthropologist during the twenty-seventh century. Her name was Tia and she was attempting to negotiate a truce between a barbaric primitive tribe called the Hecow and a more spiritual pacifistic group known as the Saleans.

---

1   Goldberg, 1988.

CHAPTER 5

Negotiations broke down and the Hecow were preparing to attack and annihilate the Saleans the following morning. Tia was in a state of panic. Not only was she about to fail on her first major assignment, but she was about to witness the massacre of a group of loving, peaceful souls.

The Higher Self of Tia's supervisor Nahill came to Tia's aid as the solution presented consisted of an astral plane negotiation during the sleep (REM or dream) state. The Saleans were very proficient at this type of OBE, as they meditated most of the day and lived the lifestyle of a current-day high priest in Tibet.

The astral negotiation worked and the Hecow were appropriately reprogrammed to leave the Saleans alone. Tia and her team joined the Saleans during this astral trip. The following morning the Hecow met with the Saleans and a lasting peace was established. This example of conscious dying had a political application.

The Higher Self is anything you want it to be, and is available whenever you desire it. Data from NDEs and "angelic" encounters provide ample support for this statement.

Our Higher Self is our chief advisor. It is quite different from the concept of Masters and Guides. These latter consultants are souls who have perfected themselves and have decided to remain in the karmic cycle (the lower five planes) to assist others in their eventual ascension (see chapter 3). These Masters and Guides are not us and we will never be them. What I mean by this is that they have a different energy source. We may have known them personally in past lives when they also possessed a karmic cycle, but they are not "genetically" related to us.

There is no death. There is only a shift in awareness. Because change alone bears rule over us, our only enemy is our own ego (our defense mechanisms). Jesus, Buddha, and others have tried to show us how to reunite ourselves with our Higher Selves. Conscious dying techniques, whether by meditation or hypnosis, assist in the connection and pave the way for our own eventual peaceful transition.

...the new physics
clearly states
that nothing exists as real
unless we observe it

CHAPTER 6

Consciousness

I n this chapter we will discuss contrasting views of consciousness, a
topic evolving from the concept of the Higher Self introduced in the
previous chapter. The Higher Self is, after all, pure consciousness. Conscious dying is a type of out-of-body experience (OBE) that I term a
"conscious out-of-body experience" (COBE). In addition, the whole
purpose of conscious dying is to maintain an unbroken connection
between the soul and the Higher Self at the exact moment of death.

THE PERENNIAL PHILOSOPHY

Godfrey Leibniz (1646–1716) coined the term "Philosophical Peren-
nis," but this philosophy was made popular with Aldous Huxley's book
The Perennial Philosophy (1944).[1] Mysticism was a key theme throughout this work.

Mysticism is defined as an expression of an inner wisdom obtained
through an altered state of consciousness (ASC). This ASC merges the
individual with the oneness of the universe. All of the major religions

1   Aldous Huxley, *The Perennial Philosophy* (New York: Ayer Publishing, 1944).

of the world include mysticism as a component. Even the most primitive religions (shamanism, for example) describe mystical experiences and incorporate them into their theology.

Most religions are literally based on accounts of these mystical encounters. The use of rituals, sacred books, and pageantry is but an attempt of these theocracies to present reports in terms that the average parishioner can comprehend. Huxley found a common core to these dogmas and he termed this the "Perennial Philosophy," which he defined as the transcendental essence of all the main religions presented through their mystical traditions.

Since these mystical experiences are entirely subjective, neither science nor religion can validate or invalidate them. It is merely a matter of faith. The Perennial Philosophy is the result of these reported encounters. The mystic is attempting to relate an experience in a language tied to his/her definition of reality. This is often, if not always, very different from that of the experience itself. For that reason, Huxley admits that it is not possible to accurately express the Perennial Philosophy.

An Absolute Ground, the reality of all things, is described in all religions' Perennial Philosophy. The Absolute is not just in all things; all things are the Absolute. The universe is only one manifestation of this Absolute. Its concept is unlimited and indefinable. Thus, the Absolute Ground is not set apart as a kind of creator separated from that which is created.

The basic concept espoused by the Perennial Philosophy is that the eternal self is united with the Absolute, and each soul is on a voyage to discover that and be enlightened. Each individual's path through life is to fulfill his or her destiny and thereby to return to his or her true home. This is accomplished through remembering our true nature rather than through learning. This is also the purpose and mechanism of conscious dying.

Ken Wilber, a current authority on the Perennial Philosophy, has compiled a common framework that underlies all experience and gives a spiritual dimension to that part of it that we call reality. Wilber refers to the lowest level of consciousness as "insentient consciousness." This level is the most dense expression of consciousness. As we ascend to the levels of consciousness, the less dense the levels become.

It is focus that separates these levels. As we go to higher levels the focus expands. Limitation of focus is why the lower planes of consciousness are not aware of those above them. Consciousness only needs to broaden its focus to ascend up this hierarchy to a new level (plane). Thus we as individuals create the very boundaries that limit our focus. Wilber describes six levels of consciousness:

1. Physical: nonliving matter/energy.

2. Biological: living (sentient) matter/energy.

3. Mental: ego, logic, thinking.

4. Subtle: archetypal, trans-individual, intuitive.

5. Causal: formless radiance, perfect transcendence.

6. Ultimate: consciousness as such, the source and nature of all other levels.[2]

Each level includes yet transcends all lower levels. The higher level is neither derived nor explained by the lower level.

Wilber subdivides each level of consciousness into a "deep structure" and a "surface structure." The deep structure contains all the potentials of that level, along with all its limits. In essence, the deep structure is a paradigm, and as such it contains the whole set of forms for that level. The limiting principles within the deep structure determine which surface structures are actualized. Wilber defines the ground subconscious as all the deep structures of all the levels existing as potentials ready to emerge. In a sense, each deep structure contains the potential of all deep structures in an enfolded order. The surface structure of a level of consciousness is a particular manifestation of the deep structure.

---

2. Ken Wilber, ed., *The Holographic Paradigm and Other Paradoxes* (Boulder, CO: Shambhala Publications, 1982), p. 157.

The difference between the deep structure and the surface structure can be illustrated by its separation from space and time. The deep structure does not have such a separation and is interconnected. The surface structure, on the other hand, is separated with a space-time attribute and is present in our physical plane.

Transformation is the term Wilber applies to the movement from one deep structure to another. The self, or level of consciousness, is doing the moving from one level to another. Its attributes are indefinable. It is the source of reality and it is the top level of consciousness, at the same time representing all levels. Wilber labels this mechanism the Atman project.

The Atman project is the child of more sophisticated levels of consciousness, also indefinable. Ascension is the manner in which the self rises up the ladder to pure consciousness. The goal is to arrive at the top layer (Atman, the God plane, ALL THAT IS, Nirvana or Heaven). The self is only limited by its ignorance of this paradigm.

By ascending levels the self can utilize its increasing powers of creativity (creating its own reality) on the mental plane. The self is constrained only by the deep structure of the material world and is conditioned by the history of such translations. Its functions are then only constrained by the deep structure of the next higher level. The only exception is level one—when operating on the physical level the self is limited by the deep structure of that level.

The self thus acts in a way to integrate levels. By identifying with at least two levels, the self becomes aware of the differences between them. This recognition allows it to break away from the lower level and ascend to the higher one.

The second or biological level is the first one to display life. Very simple biological systems such as cells and simple tissues represent this level. Not until we reach level three do we find the human mind. For the human mind to function on this mental level (level three), it must integrate the biological level beneath it. This level (level two) in turn integrates the material level (level one).

ALTERED STATES OF CONSCIOUSNESS (ASC)

Since ASCs form the basis of these mystical experiences (conscious dying can be considered mystical by any definition), let us examine this phenomenon in detail.

ASC is defined as any mental state that can be identified subjectively as sufficiently different from the general norms for that person during alert, waking consciousness. Such characteristics as changes in the character of thought and greater preoccupation than usual with internal sensations typify this state.

There are certain variables that play a significant part in the production of ASCs. Such factors are:

- Reduction of exteroceptive stimulation and/or motor activity. The continual exposure to repetitive, monotonous stimulation, and a change in the pattern and the amount of sensory input bring this about. Examples of this category are solitary confinement, highway hypnosis, extreme boredom, sensory deprivation states, and dreaming.

- Increase of exteroceptive stimulation and/or motor activity and/or emotion. Extreme emotional arousal, mental fatigue, and sensory bombardment typify this group. Examples of this type are brainwashing, religious conversion and faith healing, trance states during shamanic ceremonies, spirit possession, and acute psychotic states (such as schizophrenia).

- Increased alertness or mental involvement. A focused hyper-alertness followed by a peripheral hypoalertness over a period of time brings about this type. Sentry duty, listening to a metronome, praying, problem solving, and listening to a dynamic speaker are illustrations of this category.

- Decreased alertness or relaxation of critical faculties. Grouped under this classification are free associative states during psychoanalytic therapy, mystical states (e.g., satori, nirvana, cosmic consciousness, samadhi) reached through meditation, self hypnosis, and creative and insight states.

- Presence of somatopsychological factors. Mental states resulting from alterations in body chemistry or neurophysiology
  cause this type of ASC. Examples include auras preceding
  migraines or epileptic seizures, hyperglycemia, hypoglycemia
  following fasting, sleep deprivation, hyperventilation, and
  narcolepsy. Drugs such as psychedelics, sedatives, narcotics,
  and stimulants also produce this form of ASC.

Common Features of ASC

- Alterations in thinking. Subjective interruptions in memory, judgment, attention, and concentration characterize this
  feature.

- Disturbed time sense. Common to this are subjective feelings
  of time coming to a standstill, feelings of timelessness, and the
  slowing or acceleration of time.

- Loss of control. Someone experiencing an ASC may fear that
  he or she is losing grip on reality and losing their self-control.
  Being overtly influenced by a powerful persona is an example
  of this.

- Change in emotional expression. Displays of more intense
  and primitive emotional expressions that are sudden and
  unexpected appear. Emotional detachment may also be
  exhibited at this time.

- Body image change. A sense of depersonalization, derealiza-
  tion, and a loss of boundaries between self and others or the
  universe are observed. These encounters can be called "expansion of consciousness," or feelings of "oneness" in a mystical
  or religious setting. Not only may various parts of the body
  appear or feel shrunken, enlarged, distorted, heavy, weightless, disconnected, strange, or funny, but spontaneous experiences of dizziness, blurring of vision, weakness, numbness,
  tingling, and analgesia are likewise encountered.

- Perceptual distortions. Hallucinations, increased visual
  imagery, and various types of illusions typify this category.

- Change in meaning or significance. Feelings of profound insight, illumination, and truth are frequently observed in ASC.

- Sense of the ineffable. People who experience an ASC appear unable to communicate the essence of their experience to someone who has not had one. Amnesia is also noted.

- Feelings of rejuvenation. A new sense of hope, joy, and purpose is exhibited by the experiencer.

Applications of ASCs

- Healing. The rites and techniques performed by shamans during a healing ceremony illustrate the generation of an ASC in the patient as well as the practitioner. The early Egyptian and Greek practices of "incubation" in their sleep temples, the faith cures at Lourdes and other religious shrines, the healing through prayer and meditation, cures by the "healing touch," the laying on of hands, encounters with religious relics, spiritual healing, spirit possession cures, exorcism, mesmeric or magnetic treatment, and modern-day hypnotherapy are all obvious instances of the role of ASCs in treatment.

- Avenues of new knowledge or experience. In the realm of religion, intense prayer, passive meditation, revelatory and prophetic states, mystical and transcendental experiences, religious conversion, and divination states have served humanity in opening new realms of experience, reaffirming moral values, resolving emotional conflicts, and often enabling us to cope better with our human predicament and the world about us. Creative insights and problem solving during these states have greatly facilitated our technological advancement.

- Social function. Spirit possession, for example, would allow a priest to attain high status through fulfilling his cult role, gain a temporary freedom of responsibility from his actions and pronouncements, or enable him to act out in a socially sanctioned way his aggressive and sexual conflicts or desires. The resulting dissipation in fears and tension could easily supplant the despair and hopelessness of a difficult existence. This shows how society creates methods of reducing stress and isolation through group action.

Thus, I feel it is no "coincidence" that we humans were given this great power known as an ASC. Conscious dying is but one type of ASC that humankind can use grow spiritually.

CONSCIOUSNESS AND THE NEW PHYSICS

The American Association for the Advancement of Science formally addressed this issue in a 1979 symposium titled "The Role of Consciousness in the Physical World." SRI's Willis Harman proclaimed that the data then in hand could only be explained if scientists presupposed four key axioms concerning human consciousness and its attributes. Harman's axioms proposed that mind is spatially extended (the extensive aspect); that mind is temporally extended (the protensive aspect); that mind is ultimately dominant over the physical (the psychodynamic aspect); and that minds are joined (the concatenative aspect). Reject any of these axioms, and the data becomes inexplicable.

Beyond space-time we find pure consciousness. We cannot fathom its nature, but neither can we deny its imposing presence. This duality has led to a scientific impasse. Survey the panoply of inexplicable phenomena recorded in the literature: psychokinesis, bending light by thought, materialization and dematerialization, astral travel, out-of-body travel, clairvoyance and precognition, reincarnation, auric fields around living things, telepathy, psychometry, teleportation, levitation, healing with the mind or hands, etc.

Quantum physics, the new physics, placed a rather large fly in the ointment of our nineteenth-century mechanized view of the universe. The new physics states that reality is not fixed, and even the physical nature of matter is questionable. Consciousness is very much a component of quantum physics, whereas it played no part in the Newtonian model. Our universe today is neither objective (independent of an observer) nor determined (predictable). Nothing is real until it is observed, according to modern physics.

The paradox is this: we need particles of matter to make up the objects of our everyday world (including us), and we need an object in that very everyday world (us) to define and observe those particles. Observation implies consciousness. Therefore, consciousness is a part of the mathematical equation.

The previous laws of Newton and Maxwell showed a predictable universe. Every cause had an effect. Every effect had a cause. The past and future could be deduced if one knew the initial conditions of a state. Consciousness was explained as an epiphenomenon of the underlying structure of elementary particles and the forces between them.

In expressing the view of his time that physics was essentially complete, a leading theoretical physicist, William Thompson (Lord Kelvin), noted only two exceptions: the failure to detect the ether and the failure to understand black-body radiation (a body that absorbs all radiation falling on it). The black-body radiation problem led to quantum mechanics (dealing with subatomic particles), and the negative results of the Michaelson-Morley experiment (failure to detect the ether) led to Einstein's theory of relativity—the foundation of modern physics. Classical physics was thereby reduced to a special case of these new, more encompassing principles.

Since the observer's frame of reference had to be considered, consciousness was introduced into quantum physics equations. The well-known quantum physicist Fred Alan Wolf states:

> Classical physics holds that there is a real world out there, acting independently of human consciousness. Consciousness, in this view, is to be constructed from real objects, such as neurons and molecules. It is a byproduct of the material causes which produce the many physical effects observed.
>
> Quantum physics indicates that this theory cannot be true—the effects of observation "couple" or enter into the real world whether we want them to or not. The choices made by an observer alter, in an unpredictable manner, the real physical

events. Consciousness is deeply and inextricably involved in this picture, not a byproduct of materiality.[3]

Consciousness was not considered strictly as particles but could appear as either waves or particles. This explains remote viewing experiments during which the wave aspect of consciousness of the individual having an OBE can travel distances and recall precisely what was observed.

Quantum physics was first collectively studied in Copenhagen during the 1920s. What emerged from that conference was the concept that no quantum event occurs until it is observed. All events exist in "potentia" (Heisenberg's term) but it is the consciousness of the observer that brings it into what we refer to as reality.

This does cause a problem with those advocates of the big bang theory on the creation of our universe. This theory postulates that our universe began approximately fifteen billion years ago when some initial state with tremendous density exploded and produced our universe. Humans did not come on the scene until very recently, so how could this explanation be plausible with modern physics? It isn't. The new physics rejects this hypothesis and clearly states that nothing exists as real until we observe it.

3. Fred Alan Wolf. *The Body Quantum: The New Physics of Body, Mind and Health* (New York: Macmillan Pub Co., 1986), p. 257.

To deal with bereavement
with understanding
and empowerment…
is a sign of the soul's growth

CHAPTER 7

Death and the New Physics

Since the modern concept of time is that it does not flow, we must alter our concepts of death. The new physics has turned upside down the former concept of linear time. No physical experiment has ever been performed that detects the passage of time. It is the relativity and quantum mechanics notion of time—not the traditional Newtonian concept—that I am referring.

Thus, our view of death is inconsistent with this definition of time. Time is dependent on our consciousness, which is subjective, and therefore time cannot be demonstrated scientifically (except in the subatomic world). Modern man still has difficulty in accepting this. It is our mind that supposes time to be flowing. Nature doesn't. We serially perceive events that simply "are," and the serial perception of many such events eventuates in what we interpret to be an indisputable fact of nature, the flow of time.

The fault lies in our tendency to rely on common sense in formulating our views on death. This is equally foolish since none of us have any memories of dying, unless we are consciously reborn. The only exception is NDE, but many people still look for other ways to write off that type of "firsthand" experience. Einstein once described common sense as the deposit of prejudices laid down in the human mind before the age of eighteen.

Death is a part of the natural world as much as is life, and when science speaks about the natural world, which includes the phenomenon of time (and, therefore, death), we must listen to what is said. We cannot pick and choose, extracting only those modern scientific views we find convenient. We must look at the complete picture science gives us; therefore, we cannot ignore what the new physics has revealed to us about the nature of time.

Thanatology is a respected science today. This "death and dying" discipline has accumulated a considerable following among lay people, in addition to health professionals. Several professional journals deal with death topics. Medical schools train future doctors in this art. Death is discussed in society today far more than ever before.

Even with all this "openness" about death, the notion of flowing linear time still persists. The only single event is the universe itself. Psychologist Lawrence LeShan formulated a view of birth, life, and death around a non-linear time concept using quantum physics.[1]

He observed that birth and death demarcates life at both ends, forming boundaries to life. Noting that time in the modern sense cannot be bounded, he deduced that death as a finality was inconsistent with a modern world view. He incorporated other concepts such as field theory to build a logical case for survival of death.

As impressive as his theory is, most people will deny the possibility of attempting to reason death away. Our history is filled with examples of radically new ideas that were mocked at first, but then finally accepted. Copernicus' solar system as compared to that of Ptolemy, the evolutionary concepts of Darwin, and the change from classical Newtonian physics to quantum physics are but a few examples. Heraclitus said it best, "The only constant thing is change."

---

1   Lawrence LeShan, *The Medium, the Mystic and the Physicist* (New York: Viking Press, 1974).

Most people stay with linear time as an accepted concept, I feel, to avoid chaos. If the average person could not parcel out time as past, present, and future, in neat little boxes, the result would be panic. Are not these the divisions we use to evaluate sanity? If someone lives in the past or future, they are considered psychotic.

Even quantum physicists reportedly ignore the concept of time. They ponder this all day in their laboratories, but in their personal lives they regress back to a linear time mentality in their day-to-day behavior.

Einstein was a definite exception to this observation. He most certainly practiced what he preached. Einstein thanked his friend Michele Besso for his assistance in Einstein's work with the theory of relativity. They both worked in the patent office in Bern. This friendship lasted many years.

Besso died in 1955 and Einstein wrote the following letter to Besso's son and sister:

> The foundation of our friendship was laid in our student years in Zurich, where we met regularly at musical evenings....Later the Patent Office brought us together. The conversations during our mutual way home were of unforgettable charm....And now he has preceded me briefly in bidding farewell to this strange world. This signifies nothing. For us believing physicists the distinction between past, present, and future is only an illusion, even if a stubborn one.[2]

I trust this example illustrates the fact that we can use the principles of the new physics in our own lives for spiritual growth. To deal with bereavement with understanding and empowerment, rather than the typical "knee-jerk" emotional response, is a sign of the soul's growth. This is also one of the many advantages of conscious dying. It is a "path with a heart" as Castaneda's Don Juan might say.[3]

---

2   Banesh Hoffmann and Helen Dukas, *Albert Einstein, Creator and Rebel* (New York: Plume Books, 1973), p. 257.
3   Carlos Castenada, *Journey to Ixtlan: The Lessons of Don Juan* (New York: Simon & Schuster, 1972).

Einstein's personal philosophical and spiritual transformation based on the new physics is applicable to us all. By changing our previous prejudices toward a finality definition of death we can allow ourselves to spiritually evolve and create our own positive reality. This is not just a good idea; quantum physics mathematically and experimentally demonstrates this as fact.

If Einstein's legacy results in us overcoming our fears of death, his work would be far more important than merely splitting the atom. Our views of death have been incorrect because they were based on two false hypotheses. We assume that our body can be localized in space as one might pinpoint a rock. This is in conflict with the dynamic relationship of living things with the universe in which they function.

All particles can only be described in terms of their relationships with other particles. No one element stands by itself. The Heisenberg Uncertainty Principle in quantum physics clearly demonstrates that we cannot precisely know both the path and the location of a subatomic particle at any one moment. As we determine one of these factors, it is at the expense of the other. Since our bodies are made up of these particles, how can we justify isolating ourselves from this principle?

The second false assumption is that death must be the end of "something." The problem is this something. If it is consciousness, we have already discussed the error of this assumption in the previous chapter. The basic unit of consciousness, according to the quantum physicist Evan Harris Walker, is the quantum itself.

My purpose here is to open up your mind. Consider the philosophies from the East. Weigh them against the new physics of the West. You will note they are merging together, not moving in opposite directions.

*Memories are the only
real gift a parent
can bestow
on their children*

CHAPTER 8

The Stages of Dying

Elizabeth Kübler-Ross in 1969 published her international best sell-er, *On Death and Dying* (Macmillan). In this classic book on thana-tology, she lists five stages of dying. These stages are:

1. *Denial and Isolation*. During this stage, patients refuse to accept the hard fact that they are going to die. They also tend to iso-late themselves from their family and friends. "No, not me, this can't be true. Leave me alone."

2. *Anger*. Feelings of anger, envy, rage and resentment dominate this stage. "Why me? Why couldn't it be someone else?" This stage is most difficult for the patient accustomed to being in control of his or her life.

3. *Bargaining*. "If I ask God nicely, maybe he won't take me at this time." The patient is now desperate for anything that will extend her or his life. Often a self-imposed deadline (a wed-ding, graduation, birthday, etc.) is set by the patient with a promise not to ask for anything else.

4. *Depression*. The patient now is overwhelmed by a great sense of loss. This preparatory mood level is associated with the realization that death will take place soon. "I wish I had done more with my life."

5. *Acceptance*. This is a "numb" stage characterized by decreasing interests in the outside world and a desire to be left alone. The patient now acquiesces to the reality of his or her pending death. "I just cannot fight this battle anymore."

People do not always follow this classic pattern from denial to the anger stage, to bargaining, to depression, and finally to acceptance. It is not uncommon for two or more of these stages to surface simultaneously. They may not even occur in the proper order. When the patient has reached the stage of acceptance, yet regresses to one of the other stages, we must examine our inability to let them go, for it is this clinging on our part that is most likely responsible. This may be brought about by unnecessary life-extending devices or relatives who project guilt on the patient for leaving them at this time. This principle applies only to the acceptance stage.

Loved ones can assist the dying patient in the application of conscious dying techniques. That is my highest recommendation, of course, but for those members of the patient's social network the information in this chapter may prove helpful in assisting both the dying patient and the family in their own spiritual growth.

Instead of judging a patient in the anger stage, if we learn to assist them, then their passage to the bargaining stage will be hastened. Remember, the patient will try to "put his house in order" long before he admits, "this is happening to me."

Informing the patient of just how serious the illness is should be the responsibility of the physician. If the doctor will not relay this news to the patient, then someone else must; the patient has a right to know if death is imminent. A family member can and should assume this role.

Dying patients should not be treated with pity. They are human beings and at times may want to talk, or in other more private instances being alone may be indicated. Occasionally, the person may simply ask you to sit by them and hold their hand. If you don't know what to say, try "Is this difficult for you?" or "Is there anything I can do for you?"

It is easy for a dying patient to deny their condition. In chapter 4, I point out society's general denial of death. Once both the family and the patient face and accept their physical finiteness, life then becomes more meaningful and more valuable. At this time I am not dealing with our immortality and the conscious dying process.

Caretakers (see chapter 17) often feel frustrated when they face the anger of a dying patient. Your first response to this should be an investigation of the justification for their anger. If it can be rectified, then by all means correct the situation. However, if this is the classic "why me?" anger stage, let them know that you can understand their anger and would be equally upset if you were in their position. By allowing them to ventilate their anguish without fostering feelings of guilt or belittling them, you are helping them grow and deal with their situation. You will grow also.

Another syndrome to note is partial death. Elderly patients in nursing homes and hospitals who are "vegetating" and merely existing are in this situation. They may not have caring families and, since they feel they have no future, a giving-up stance is taken. Every person has something to contribute if we would only permit its manifestation. The family does have a responsibility to lend their love and support to these patients and give them a chance.

Thanatologists have long observed that the true values of life can be learned from dying patients. If the average person could attain the stage of acceptance at a young age, a more meaningful life could be lived.

Another consideration is a sudden accidental death or suicide. It is critical that the family view the body. No matter how mutilated the corpse may appear, it is important for the family to view at least part of an identifiable body in order to come to grips with the reality of the death. Failure to do so can lead to a general state of denial lasting many years.

It is also important to understand the dying patient's view of hope. Two aspects of hope may be exhibited. Hope for a cure of their illness and prolongation of life surfaces in the beginning. This also is felt by the family and hospital personnel. Eventually this hope evolves into the second type, characterized by hope for life after death or concern for those being left behind. It is crucial that we listen to the patient and not project our own feelings or fears onto them. We cannot help them if we do.

A parent with a terminal illness has a responsibility to discuss their situation with each of their children, preferably individually. The patient needs to prepare them, especially if they are young children. If we could live each day as if it were the last one, this would facilitate more enjoyment of each and every moment. Memories are the only real gifts parents can bestow on their children.

For the surviving family, guilt is the most common result of the death of a loved one. "If only I had called the doctor earlier" is a frequent statement made by family members. They need to be reassured that they most likely did everything that was indicated. Relatives commonly feel this guilt due to past angry wishes and actions toward the recently departed. This unresolved anger can be quite destructive and may result in psychosomatic illness if left untreated.

The main point I am trying to make in this chapter is that death is a circumstance that needs to be dealt with openly. We do more harm by avoiding or disguising the issue than by using this time to share with and listen to the patient. Society's denial of death has not prepared us properly to deal with this most significant time of life.

As long as the patient is aware of our willingness to take the extra time to listen and sit with him or her, we will notice a reaction of increased hope and relief in their demeanor. By becoming sensitive to the needs of the terminally ill patient you are facilitating both responses, key components to a peaceful transition.

*...it is possible for consciousness
to exist apart from the physical body...
suggesting that consciousness
could survive death*

CHAPTER 9

The Out-of-Body Experience

Since the conscious dying (COBE) experience is a type of out-of-body experience (OBE), a detailed discussion of this phenomenon will be the topic of this chapter. I have already discussed NDEs in detail in chapter 2, so this chapter will deal with those OBEs (see chapter 1) that predominantly do not involve a clinical death or response to a time of extreme distress.

Years ago the term "astral projection" was used to describe OBEs. At that time most experiencers of this phenomenon were reticent to discuss it. They feared being ridiculed or even labeled as insane, though many thousands of such experiences have been noted.

One evening while lying in her bedroom and listening to chamber music performed by her husband and friends downstairs, Mrs. Caroline Larsen stated:

> "A feeling of deep depression and apprehension came over me
> ... and soon a numbness crept over me until every muscle
> became paralyzed....The next thing I knew was that I was

standing on the floor beside my bed looking down attentively at my own physical body laying on it."[1]

This Vermont housewife walked downstairs in her "astral body" and sat in on the gathering of musicians. Later she returned to her physical body and her husband confirmed the details of what his wife told him, even though no one was aware of her presence.

The scientist does not place much credence on anecdotal reports such as these, but one observation that has often been reported is the presence of a silver cord connecting the physical body to the astral one.

A British housewife, Mrs. H. D. Williams, reported that during a spontaneous OBE she saw "a shining white cord, two or three inches wide" which "was attached to the head of my physical body."

Dr. Louisa Rhine at the Foundation for Research on the Nature of Man at Duke University stated that there appear to be three types of OBEs.[2]

The first type is described as an envelopment in an apparition form. One such subject reported:

> I was awakened by the sun shining through the door across my face and eyes. I got up to close the door…when I looked in the mirror I saw the strangest thing there. It looked like me but it was just a white vapor image of myself….When I reached my bed, there was I in bed and sound asleep. There were two of me.

Experiencing the "consciousness" of floating in space is the second type, typified by the following observation:

> I was [floating] near the ceiling of the north window that opened on the rear garden. The colors of everything were vivid and glowing. I did not see myself as having any form. Time was suspended; suddenly I was in the bed again feeling my body as heavy.

1   Robert Crookall. *More Astral Projections* (London: Aquarian Press, 1964).
2   Robert Crookall. *The Study and Practice of Astral Projection* (London: Aquarian Press, 1961).

The third type is characterized by the perceiver being devoid of a body of any kind.

> Twenty-five years ago I was seriously sick and was rushed to the hospital....I felt as though I were going to die....Finally, a little light hovered over my still form and all my senses were transferred into this small light..., I, or rather the little light, flew around the operating room watching everything that was taking place.

The first true chronology of OBEs resulted from the work of the British occultist Oliver Fox. Fox describes a classic OBE and noted that the "world" one observes during an OBE is not an exact duplicate of the physical plane. He is also noteworthy in being able to induce lucid dreaming (being aware that you are dreaming) and manipulate these "dreams of knowledge" into OBEs (see chapter 6). He wrote:

> I was lying in the bed in the afternoon when I experienced the False Awakening, imagining that my wife and two friends were sitting in the room and talking. I felt too tired to take part in any part of this conversation and "went to sleep" again. When I next became aware of my surroundings I realized that I was in the Trance Condition [catalepsy] and could leave my body. I, therefore, sat up (out-of-the-body, as it were) and then leisurely got off the bed. Dual consciousness was very strong. I could feel myself lying in the bed and standing by it, my legs pressing against the coverlet, simultaneously; though I could see all the objects in the room quite clearly, I could not see my physical body when I looked for it upon the bed. Everything seemed just as real as in waking life—more so, extra vivid—and I felt indescribably well and free, my brain seeming extraordinarily alert. I left the bed and walked slowly around the room to the door, the sense of dual consciousness diminishing as I moved farther away from the body; but just as I was going to leave the room, my body pulled me back instantaneously and the trance was broken.[3]

---

3   Oliver Fox. *Astral Projection* (London: University Books, 1962).

Sylvan Muldoon of America described many OBEs. His most significant contribution was his depiction of the "silver cord." This cord linked the physical and astral bodies. It became thinner as he moved farther away from his physical body. Less and less consciousness was felt as the silver cord was stretched.

Muldoon, unlike Fox, could actually affect physical matter during an OBE. He reported overturning a mattress and setting a metronome in motion.

Among other chronicles of OBE are: Marcel-Louis Forhan, a French mystic who traveled extensively in China, wrote his experiences under the pen name of Yram, in a book translated as *Practical Astral Projection;* Cora Richmond, an American psychic, wrote her autobiography as *My Experiments Out of the Body*; Vincent Turvey, a British psychic and spiritualist in his *The Beginnings of Seership*. Others such as William Dudley Pelley and Mrs. Shine Gifford had complex single experiences which they wrote up in booklet form.

Professor J. H. M. Whiteman, a professor of mathematics at Capetown University, detailed his OBEs in his book *The Mystical Life*. Whiteman points out that the percipient enters into a non-physical replica of the physical world. It is the conditioned perception of the subject that controls the form and structure of this astral dimension. As the observer orients to this non-physical plane, the perception of this world changes and it becomes more mystical.

Whiteman perceived himself in some type of "form" during an OBE and noted a "tugging" at the back of the head when he finally returned to the physical body. He described "visual and circular openings" during the beginning of the experience.

> The separation began with a 'special opening' in which the surface of a whitewashed wall, two feet away, was studied, with a full clarity of perception and the visual impressions of precise special position and of seeing "through the eyelids" of the physical eyes, which remained consciously shut. The opening then changed to one in which heath-like country was seen in a wide panorama, with steep ground in front, and almost at once

I was conscious for a few moments of being catapulted and amidst that scene.[4]

Common characteristics reported by OBE subjects include:

- Sensations of leaving and re-entering the physical body.

- The experience of dual consciousness when near the physical body.

- Colors are perceived more vividly, as are objects.

- Scenes of unexplainable beauty are noted. These are often unrelated to the physical environment.

- Feelings of "tuggings" at the back of the head when the OBE is too long in duration. This precedes the return to the physical body.

- The astral world is usually somewhat different from the physical world.

Fox wrote about an interesting verification of an OBE. His girlfriend Elsie told him she would project her astral body to his room one evening. As she had never visited his room, Fox was amazed when Elsie described its layout the following day.

Laboratory experiments demonstrating this remote viewing were begun by S. H. Beard. Beard was a friend of Edmund Gurney, one of the pioneers of the Society for Psychical Research. Gurney detailed Beard's research in a book titled *Phantasms of the Living*.

Eleanor Sidgwick, another pioneer of this society, published an account of Mrs. Wilmot in the former's paper "On the Evidence for Clairvoyance," published in the *Proceedings* of the Society for Psychical Research. One evening in Bridgeport, Connecticut, Mrs. Wilmot was very worried about her husband's safety during an ocean crossing of the Atlantic in stormy weather. She had an OBE and materialized on the ship and kissed her husband in full view of his cabin mate. This man, William Tait, teased Mr. Wilmot about his "girlfriend" and about

---

4 Hornell Hart. "Scientific Survival Research," *Inter. Journal of Parapsychology* 9, 1967: 43–52.

informing his wife of the incident. Later when Mrs. Wilmot and Tait compared notes, several mutually corroborative items appeared.

It was not until the 1960s that two eminent scientists, Robert Crookall and Charles Tart, made their contributions to OBE research. Dr. Crookall collected nearly one thousand reports from firsthand accounts sent to him and the scientific literature. His books include: *The Study and Practice of Astral Projection, More Astral Projections,* and *Case-book of Astral Projection.*[5]

Crookall details four different types of analysis of his data. The first is based on "Whatley's Law of Evidence." This principle states that if enough independent witnesses who could not have consorted together to falsify a report agree upon the characteristics of an observation, then the observation has a high likelihood of being true. Six primary traits surfaced: (1) The percipient feels that he is leaving the physical body through the head. (2) A blackout occurs at the moment of separation of consciousness from the body. (3) The apparitional body hovers above the physical body. (4) The apparitional body resumes this position before the termination of the experience. (5) A blackout occurs at the moment of reintegration. (6) Rapid re-entry causes shock to the physical body.

Other observations included seeing other apparitions, ESP, and the presence of a silver cord.

Crookall's second analysis revealed that spontaneous OBEs were more vivid and had different characteristics than those that had been forced (NDE, drug induced, etc.). His third analysis showed that psychics reported experiences similar to the forced type, whereas non-psychic individuals reported the profile of spontaneous OBEs. In the fourth analysis Crookall observed that many OBEs occur in two stages. An initial state of confusion characterized the initial stage of an OBE. At the end of these OBEs, the subject exhibited a clearing of consciousness and a vagueness in the return to the physical body.

---

5   All published by Citadel Press, Carol Publishing Group, New York, in 1966, 1964, and 1973, respectively.

Charles Tart has added significantly to OBE research. As an experimental psychologist at the University of California at Davis, he monitored OBEs by following brain-wave (EEG) patterns in the controlled setting of a laboratory. Tart's first subject, Robert Monroe, demonstrated REM (rapid eye movements, indicative of dreaming) and correctly exhibited remote viewing. Monroe (now deceased) later wrote his own books, such as *Journeys Out of the Body*, which detailed this research.[6]

By his subjects reading notes and number combinations placed in rooms physically separate from the laboratory, this remote viewing evidence proved significant in advancing this most unusual phenomenon from a scientific perspective. Other examples of remote viewing experiments can be found in the work of Russell Targ at Stanford Research Institute (SRI) in the 1970s and 1980s. Here the U.S. Department of Defense spent millions of taxpayer dollars on OBE research.

The study of OBE has emerged from its anecdotal beginnings to the domain of scientific experimentation. OBE research demonstrates that it is possible for consciousness to exist apart from the physical body. This suggests that consciousness could indeed survive death. Some of Tart's EEG readings mimic those of meditators, suggesting a commonality in these "mystical" experiences. Lastly, the ESP so often noted during an OBE almost leaves the impression that the mind purposely utilizes this state in order to gather information not readily available to the physical body.

LUCID DREAMING

In lucid dreaming the dreamer is aware of being in the dream state. Often they are able to direct the outcome of the dream. Stephan LaBerge at the Stanford Medical Center has conducted the most extensive research in this field. He states that we control the dream's content in this state. Lucid dreaming is used by the subjects of LaBerge's experiments to find solutions to everyday problems. Their lucid dreams

---

6   Robert Monroe. *Journeys Out of the Body* (New York: Doubleday, 1973).

function as a form of simulation of different scenarios and are a form of out-of-body experiences.

LaBerge calls his method the "Mnemonic Induction of Lucid Dreams" or MILD. In addition to a strong motivation to have a lucid dream, LaBerge outlines his technique in four steps in his book titled *Lucid Dreaming*:[7]

1. At some point in the early morning when you have awakened spontaneously from a dream, quickly go over every detail of the dream in your mind and repeat the process several times until you have completely memorized the dream.

2. Then, while you are still lying in bed, repeat to yourself several times, "Next time I'm dreaming, I want to remember to recognize that I'm dreaming."

3. After repeating this phrase, picture yourself back in the dream you just finished dreaming, only imagining that this time you realize that you are dreaming.

4. Keep the visualization in your mind until it is clearly fixed or you fall back to sleep.

Lucid dreaming is a very ancient practice. In Tibet the ability to be awake in one's dreams was considered a prerequisite to spiritual advancement and was known as the Yoga of the Dream State, or *Milam*. In his book *The Tantric Mysticism of Tibet*, the distinguished Orientalist and translator of the *I Ching* John Blofeld states, "In this yoga, the adept is taught to enter the dream state at will, to explore its characteristics and return to the waking state without any break in his stream of normal consciousness. Thereby he discovers the illusory nature of both states and learns how to die...and to be reborn without loss of memory."[8]

---

7   Stephan LaBerge. *Lucid Dreaming* (New York: Ballantine, 1986).
8   John Blofeld. *The Tantric Mysticism of Tibet* (Boston: Shambhala, 1987).

HEALING AND OUT-OF-BODY EXPERIENCES

A review of NDE (see chapter 2) will more than illustrate the healing effects of OBEs. Since NDE reflects unconscious dying rather than conscious dying, a study of less extreme OBEs is more fruitful in keeping with the theme of this book.

Religious healings have been documented since recorded history began. They are characterized by:

- Levitation.

- Out-of-body experience.

- Movement into extraphysical worlds during hypnosis, lucid dreams, and deep meditation.

- Deliberate influence imposed by a mind upon living tissue at a distance (telergy).

- The creation of a special joy or presence in their place of worship by mystics and saints.

Both the Old and New Testaments report several examples of these healings. My recent book, *Soul Healing*,[9] documents these in detail. Most interesting are the healings that take place at Lourdes. In 1883, twenty-five years after Bernadette Soubirous received her famous vision of the Virgin Mary at this site in France, the Catholic Church founded a medical bureau there. The bureau, along with an International Medical Committee, has documented hundreds of these miraculous healings. The recipients often describe spontaneous OBEs during their visit to this shrine.

The practice of shamanism is also indicative of conscious dying and OBE healings, except with a most unusual twist. The shaman is the one who leaves his body and goes on a search to aid an ailing patient. The "magical flights" of the shaman have been termed "ecstatic journeys" and involve a circuitous trip above and below the earth

9   Dr. Bruce Goldberg. *Soul Healing* (St. Paul, MN: Llewellyn Publications, 1996).

in search of "fugitive souls." A lost soul must be captured and returned to its rightful place within the patient's body in order for the healing to be effective.

The universe in general is conceived as having three levels—sky, earth, and underworld—connected by a central axis. This axis passes through an opening, a "hole." The hole serves as a multi-purpose vestibule: gods pass through it to descend to earth, the dead use it to reach the subterranean regions, and the soul of the shaman journeys through it in either direction while in ecstasy.

Meditation offers another example of OBE healing—the deep meditative state of "extraordinary awareness" or "nirvana" or "satori" is a form of enlightenment characterized by an OBE. This technique can be used to bring about a COBE. The detachment achieved during these states constitutes a superconscious mind tap.

Characteristics attributed to this enlightened state include:

- A positive mood (tranquility, peace of mind).

- An experience of unity or oneness with the environment; what the ancients called the joining of microcosm (man) with macrocosm (universe).

- A sense of inability to describe the experience with words.

- An alteration in time/space relationships.

- An enhanced sense of reality and meaning.

- Paradoxicality—that is, acceptance of things that seem paradoxical in ordinary consciousness.

Meditation's healing effects have been documented in the treatment of anxiety and anxiety neurosis and of phobias. It is effective for increasing "self-actualization" and "positive mental health," and as an adjunct in the treatment of drug and alcohol abuse or of essential hypertension.

The presence of yoga further illustrates this form of healing. The embodied spirit of the individual becomes one with the Universal Spirit through the regular practice of certain physical and mental exercises. These postures and psycho-physiological practices lead the individual to samadhi (suspended nervous sensation), samatua (freedom from emotions), and dharana (a focused concentration resulting in a state of detachment). Various examples of healing are reported during these COBE states.

In summary, the basic principles of OBE healing are:

- Because healing energies originate at a spiritual level, they can work on any facet of a person's being.

- The patient must be motivated and willing to experience OBE healing. Each one of us has free will to accept or reject healing energies.

- The Higher Self directs the union of the patient and OBE healer by way of energy.

- Illness is not seen as a problem to be fought against. It is a condition of imbalance of energies. The purpose of illness is to bring something to our attention.

- OBE healing cooperates with the body's own healing forces rather than overriding them.

- OBE healing is completely natural and every one of us has the ability to draw up this healing energy resource.

Part II

The Practice of
Conscious Dying

...according to the ancients
we are born
on an inhalation
and die on an exhalation

CHAPTER 10

Techniques of Conscious Dying

Your own motivation is the key to the success of this approach. The techniques are actually quite simple and anyone can apply them. You must want, in your "heart of hearts," to accomplish these goals or else nothing will avail.

Over the years, I have found that the use of cassette tapes results in the most successful experiences with hypnosis. The transcripts given in this chapter can be used as a model for you to make your own tapes.

Where the transcripts indicate the playing of New Age music, you can use whatever music you like. However, you will find metaphysical music ideal for these experiences. If you would prefer to use professionally recorded tapes, contact my office and I will be happy to send you a complete list of my pre-recorded self-hypnosis tapes.

The other option is to simply read these scripts to yourself or to another person. If this option is selected, there are some methods that will help maximize this experience. These are:

1. Read with purpose and confidence.

2. Deliver your reading with enthusiasm.

3. Read slowly and distinctly.

4. Read every script as if it is critical to the life of the recipient.

5. Read each script as if you had just composed them.

6. Read the scripts as if it were for the first time.

7. Read these scripts at the same time each day.

8. In doing the meditation scripts practice with the general meditation exercise a few times by itself before you try the before death and after-death meditations.

9. When you are ready to do the before-death meditation, use the general meditation first as a conditioning and lead in to the before-death meditation. When doing this, ignore the instruction to play New Age music for 15 minutes in the general meditation script.

10. The same technique mentioned in step 9 applies to the use of the after-death meditation script.

11. The room in which meditation is to be practiced should be dimly lit, and a few degrees above room temperature. You should allow about twenty minutes to use the scripts.

The Western definition of meditation involves concentrating on something. Easterners would describe this same state as a transcending of all conceptual thinking to attain a state of pure consciousness.

Meditation itself is a form of conscious dying in that the conscious mind proper (small m) dies, while the subconscious and superconscious mind (capital M) goes on living.

All traditional meditation practices deal with breathing techniques. Some procedures use a mantra, others chanting of prayers, and still others use a *koan*. A koan is a question that appears to be impossible to answer. "What is the sound of one hand clapping?" is an example of a koan. The student answers this question by focusing his or her concentration quietly for several hours.

Breath is said to connect all life with consciousness. It bridges the conscious mind proper to the subconscious. According to the ancients, we are born on an inhalation and die on an exhalation. Breath is sometimes spoken of as the pulse of the mind, suggesting a direct relationship between thinking and breathing.

The dying patient may want to recite a mantra based on his or her religion. For example, Buddhists might chant, "Om Mam Padme Hum." Christians may prefer the Jesus Prayer of the Heart: "Lord Jesus Christ, have mercy on me." The ancient "Shi'Ma" ("Hear oh Israel, the Lord our God, the Lord is one.") is often selected by Jewish patients. These prayers may precede the playing of meditation tapes and should be recited on the exhalation breath.

Do not be concerned about using these scripts word by word. It is your heart chakra that directs your meditation. Feel free to amplify and expand on these scripts. Allow your "stream of consciousness" from your Higher Self to edit these karmic scripts.

When you access the Higher Self (superconscious mind) you will observe the following:

- A positive mood (tranquility, peace of mind).

- An experience of unity or oneness with the environment, what the ancients called the joining of microcosm (man) with macrocosm (universe).

- A sense of inability to describe the experience with words.

- An alteration in time/space relationships.

- An enhanced sense of reality and meaning.

Even the ancient Hindu and Zen scriptures on meditation point out that it is far more important to *attempt* to achieve the Higher Self state than it is to actually reach that state. Simply by taking time out to meditate, the individual is making a conscious effort to improve their health. This effect, by definition, is the opposite of the behavior pattern that leads to excessive stress. The importance of simply meditating, rather than achieving the superconscious state, will remove much of the competitive, or success-versus-failure component in this process.

GENERAL MEDITATION SCRIPT

Focus all of your attention on your breath. Concentrate on the mechanics of breathing, not the thought of the breath. Note how it comes and goes. As the breath enters and leaves the nostrils, feel the expansion and contraction of the lungs.

Focus on the awareness of breathing. Remove all other thoughts and feelings from your awareness. Observe this natural life process. Do not try to change it. Merely be with it. Let yourself receive the changing sensations that accompany this process.

As you inhale and exhale, one breath at a time, let it happen by itself. If it is deep, let it be deep. If it is slow, let it be slow. If it is shallow, let it be shallow.

If you sense the mind is interfering with this process, just focus on the inhalation and exhalation. Be one with your breath. Nothing else matters.

Observe the uniqueness of each breath. Observe, don't analyze. Note the changing sensations. Be one with your breath.

Ignore all other functions of the body. Remove all thoughts from your mind. You are the breath. Be one with your breath.

You are now floating with the universe. As the wind carries a feather, you are being carried by your breath.

Notice how the distracting thoughts fade. How they become meaningless. All that matters is that you breathe. You are your breath. Be one with your breath.

Let go of the body. Feel as if you have no body. You are weightless, as is your breath.

You are floating in the universe. You are at peace with the universe. You are one with the universe.

Notice how relaxed you are, now that you are free of the confines of the body. You are totally one with the universe.

There is nowhere to go. Nobody is expecting you. You have no schedule or deadline. You are free. Enjoy this moment, for you are one with the universe.

Be quiet. Do not cough or make any movement or sound. Just be still and merge with the universe. You are consciousness.

Let go of all fear and doubt. Let go of all thoughts. Do not try to control your being. Just be free and one with your consciousness.

You have no body. You have no limitations. You are one with your consciousness. You are one with the universe.

Let each moment occur by itself. Observe it and enjoy these intervals of time. Do not resist this merging with your consciousness.

You are now nothing but consciousness. You are the universe.

PLAY NEW AGE MUSIC FOR 15 MINUTES

Now it is time to return to your body. Again, concentrate on your breath. Now note the other functions of your body. Slowly open up your eyes and do what you feel is important at this time.

BEFORE-DEATH MEDITATION SCRIPT

Now you are about to enter a very special journey. This is an experience that you have already prepared for many times. You have consciously died many times.

This time your preparation is guided by your Higher Self and your Masters and Guides, with your complete awareness. You are perfectly safe.

See the white light around you, protecting you so that there is no need to be concerned. Be one with the white light. You are the white light.

You are able to maintain your connection with your Higher Self at this time. You are able to keep this connection as we simulate your soul's crossing into spirit and leaving the physical body. This is conscious dying. You are always safe and protected.

You can and will be able to communicate with your Higher Self. It may be by telepathy. You can also hear sounds from the earth plane. You are protected and safe.

Look back at your physical body. Do not be concerned about it. It may be dead but you are not. You are spirit. You are soul. You are immortal. Be one with your Higher Self. Be one with your perfect energy. You are your Higher Self.

Observe the death process. Remember, you are conscious. You have died consciously. You are protected by the white light. You are perfectly safe. Your Higher Self is with you.

Leave behind all earth-plane baggage. Leave behind all fears, pain, worries, and insecurities. Immerse yourself in the protective white light coming from your Higher Self. Be one with your Higher Self.

Listen to your Higher Self. It will guide you on a fantastic journey shortly. Be open to its instructions. Have no fear. You are protected. You are perfectly safe.

Do not cling to your old physical body. Do not cling to your Higher Self either. Be empowered. Be confident. You are an evolved soul and with your Higher Self.

You are now on your way to the soul plane. Feel yourself being drawn up to the soul plane. Feel the presence of your Higher Self advising you, protecting you.

Note the changes in colors and sounds as you move toward the soul plane. See how well you have adapted to this trip. See how you avoided the disorienting forces of the lower planes. See how easy it is to do this. Be one with your Higher Self.

As you enter the soul plane observe how peaceful and organized it is. It is warm, yet efficient in helping you choose your destiny. Note how your Higher Self is with you always.

See how the selection process is done. Note how your Higher Self assists you in this choice. See the presence of your Masters and Guides as you are presented with choices on this, the soul plane.

Do not be concerned if you must return to the earth plane. Do not be concerned if you must reincarnate. You will be reborn consciously as you have died consciously. You will have a better and more spiritual life.

If you must return to a physical body this conscious rebirth will result in a spiritually evolved lifetime. It will be more fulfilling and more joyous than the life you just lived. Your Higher Self will assist you in this conscious rebirth. Be one with your Higher Self.

If you do not have to reincarnate, if you can ascend to the higher planes, rejoice, for shortly you will be with God. You will no longer need to be assisted by your Higher Self. You will be your Higher Self. You and your Higher Self have merged. You are your Higher Self.

You are your Higher Self. Rejoice. You are one with the universe. You are pure consciousness. You are the white light. You are your Higher Self.

PLAY NEW AGE MUSIC FOR 15 MINUTES

Now it is time to return to your body. Again, concentrate on your breath. Now note the other functions of your body. Slowly open up your eyes and do what you feel is important at this time.

AFTER-DEATH MEDITATION SCRIPT

Look down at your body. It has died, but you are alive. You have practiced conscious dying and now you are going to apply all that you have learned. Feel the connection with your Higher Self. Listen as it telepathically communicates with you. Listen as it assists you during this transition. Be one with your Higher Self.

No longer are your thoughts about the earth plane. No longer are your concerns for the physical body. Feel the freedom that you have earned. Keep in contact, always, with your Higher Self.

See how easy it is. It's as though you have memorized a song and are now singing along with a tape of it. It's that simple.

Feel the presence of the white light. Do not be afraid. Your Higher Self is with you, always. Your Higher Self is your true self. Merge with your Higher Self. Be one with your Higher Self. You are your Higher Self.

Leave behind all concerns, fears, and other baggage from your past life and earth. Look forward to this new exciting adventure. Feel the presence of your Higher Self. Communicate with it. Listen to its instructions. Be one with your Higher Self.

CHAPTER 10

The clinical death you just experienced is meaningless. It is like a reptile shedding its skin. The white light is your next goal. See it, feel it, move toward it.

Let your Higher Self assist you. Be open to your Higher Self. Merge with your Higher Self. Be one with your Higher Self.

Understand the truth of the universe. Your Higher Self knows this truth. Open up yourself to your Higher Self. Merge with your Higher Self. Be one with your Higher Self.

Do not cling to your previous life. Forget about it for now. You will have plenty of time to evaluate it upon your arrival on the soul plane.

Listen to the sounds around you. Your hearing is now very acute. Concentrate on being one with your experience of freedom. No longer do you have a physical body. No longer do you feel pain. No longer do you have fear. You are free.

Let your Higher Self direct you toward the white light. Be open to this experience. Look forward to this special trip. Be one with your Higher Self. You are your Higher Self.

You are about to begin a long and wonderful journey. This journey will take you to the soul plane. By carefully following these instructions you will avoid the karmic cycle.

The only energy you will be aware of is that of your Higher Self. Your Higher Self is perfect. It is pure consciousness. You are one with your Higher Self. You are pure consciousness.

As you travel to the soul plane you may meet other entities. Do not be concerned. Your Higher Self is with you. Listen to your Higher Self. Be one with your Higher Self.

These souls may be your guides, or they may be loved ones who have died before you. See how they are surrounded by white light. They too are pure consciousness.

Telepathically communicate with these souls if you meet them. Listen to their thoughts. Let your Higher Self help you. Merge with your Higher Self. Be one with your Higher Self.

Notice how far you have traveled. It is not necessary to look back. See the colors change as you move through these dimensions. Listen to the different sounds. Merge with your Higher Self. Be one with your Higher Self.

Listen to your Higher Self as it instructs you. Listen to what it has to say about your trip to the soul plane. See how much confidence it has in you. See how comfortable you feel now.

Feel the pull of the white light. It surrounds you now and gently moves you forward. You are actually traveling quite fast, but it feels as if you are on an escalator.

Note how well you have adapted to this experience. Observe how much you like communicating with your Higher Self. See how good it feels to finally be free of the body. You are one with the universe.

Just as you were not aware of your breathing when you had a physical body. Just as you did not notice each second as it elapsed on the earth plane. See how time is dimensionless. Feel how easy this trip is.

Now that you have avoided the karmic cycle feel the attraction to the soul plane ahead. Feel the presence of your Higher Self. Merge with your Higher Self. You are your Higher Self.

Now you are entering the soul plane. Observe its intricacies. Note how welcome you are here. See how much fun it is to overview all of your past and future lives. Feel the continued presence of your Higher Self.

Now, as you totally immerse yourself in the pure consciousness of the soul plane, listen carefully to your Higher Self. Your Higher Self is assisting in your transition to the Higher Planes.

You no longer have to reincarnate on the lower planes. You no longer have a karmic cycle. Bathe in this feeling of perfectness. You are perfect. Merge completely with your Higher Self. You are your Higher Self.

Prepare to ascend to the Higher Planes. You are on your way to be with God. You have graduated from the cycle of birth and death. You are one with your perfect energy.

As you ascend to the higher planes things appear different. You are a special soul, a perfect soul. There is no doubt. There is no fear. There is only truth, perfection, and beauty.

Do not be concerned with the changes in colors, sounds, and vibration. Just observe the process. You are perfect and on your way to join God. Be one with your God.

Instructions for Using the Conscious Dying Script/Tape

To prepare for this experience, I recommend:

1. Do this at a time that you will not be disturbed. Make sure that no deadline or time limit is set.

2. Lie down or place yourself in whatever position you find most conducive to relaxation. Loosen any clothing that feels tight or distracting in any way. Feel free to take off your shoes and be sure to remove any jewelry. Darken the room, but avoid a pitch-black environment.

3. Since in the COBE state you are subjected to every thought that crosses your mind, close your mind to any thoughts or focus on a single thought as best you can.

4. To facilitate leaving the physical body, think of getting lighter and of floating upward. Focus on how nice it would be to do this.

5. Keep all concentration on a single goal, one at a time. Refrain from distracting thoughts. Mentally tell yourself that you can see and communicate with your Higher Self.

6. For traveling while out of the body you must go to a person and not a place. Think not only of the person's name but of the character and personality of this individual. Do not try to visualize a physical person. Focus instead on the inner person.

7. Merely thinking of your physical body will initiate the return process. Mentally, then physically, move a finger or toe, or take a deep breath, and your soul will immediately return to the physical body. This technique is perfectly safe.

8. Open up your eyes and sit up after this re-entry. You will be able to do anything else that you have planned for the day or evening.

CONSCIOUS DYING SCRIPT: A CONSCIOUS OUT-OF-BODY EXPERIENCE (COBE)

Now listen very carefully. I want you to imagine a bright white light coming down from above and entering the top of your head, filling your entire body. See it, feel it, and it becomes reality. Now imagine an aura of pure white light emanating from your heart region. Again surrounding your entire body. Protecting you. See it, feel it, and it becomes reality. Now only your Masters and Guides, Higher Self, and highly evolved loving entities who mean you well will be able to influence you during this or any other hypnotic session. You are totally protected by this aura of pure white light.

Now as you focus in on how comfortable and relaxed you are, free of distractions, free from physical and emotional obstacles that prevent you from safely leaving and returning to the physical body, you will perceive and remember all that you encounter during this experience. You will recall in detail when you are physically awake only these matters that will be beneficial to your physical and mental being and experience. Now begin to sense the vibrations around you, and in your own mind begin to shape and pull them into a ring around your head. Do this for a few moments now.

PLAY NEW AGE MUSIC FOR 2 MINUTES

Now as you begin to attract these vibrations into your inner awareness, they begin to sweep throughout your body, making it rigid and immobile. You are always in complete control of this experience. Do this now as you perceive yourself rigid and immobile, with these vibrations moving along and throughout your entire body.

PLAY NEW AGE MUSIC FOR 2 MINUTES

You have done very well. Pulse these vibrations. Perceive yourself feeling the pulse of these vibrations throughout your entire awareness. In your own mind's eye, reach out one of your arms and grasp some object that you know is out of normal reach. Feel the object and let your astral hand pass through it. Your mind is using your astral hand, not your physical hand, to feel the object. As you do this you are becoming lighter and lighter, and your astral body is beginning to rise up from your physical body. Do this now.

PLAY NEW AGE MUSIC FOR 2 MINUTES

You've done very well. Now, using other parts of your astral body (your head, feet, chest, and back) repeat this exercise and continue to feel lighter and lighter as your astral body begins to rise up from your physical body. Do this now.

PLAY NEW AGE MUSIC FOR 2 MINUTES

Now think of yourself as becoming lighter and lighter throughout your body. Perceive yourself floating up as your entire astral body lifts up and floats away from your physical body. Concentrate on blackness and remove all fears during this process. Imagine a helium-filled balloon rising and pulling your astral body with it, up and away from your physical body. Do this now.

PLAY NEW AGE MUSIC FOR 2 MINUTES

See how easy it is to leave the body while remaining in complete contact with your Higher Self. This is the process of conscious dying. It is that simple. Now ask your Higher Self for any instruction that will assist your spiritual growth. Remember, your Higher Self is all-knowledgeable and has access to your akashic records.

Now slowly and carefully state your desire for information or an experience and let your Higher Self work for you. Let it help you raise your soul's energy.

PLAY NEW AGE MUSIC FOR 3 MINUTES

You have done very well. Now I want you to further open up the channels of communication by removing any obstacles and allowing yourself to receive information and experiences that will directly apply to and help better your present lifetime. Allow yourself to receive more advanced and more specific information from your Higher Self and Masters and

Guides to raise your frequency and improve your karmic sub-cycle. Maintain the communication and connection with your Higher Self. You are one with your Higher Self. This connection will always exist, even when the physical body dies. Allow your Higher Self to instruct you. Do this now.

PLAY NEW AGE MUSIC FOR 3 MINUTES

All right now. Sleep now and rest. You did very very well. Listen very carefully. I'm going to count forward now from 1 to 5. When I reach the count of 5 you will be back in your physical body. You will be able to remember everything you experienced and re-experienced, you'll feel very relaxed, refreshed, you'll be able to do whatever you have planned for the rest of the day or evening. You'll feel very positive about what you've just experienced and very motivated about your confidence and ability to play this tape again to experience conscious dying. All right now. 1 very, very deep, 2 you're getting a little bit lighter, 3 you're getting much much lighter, 4 very, very light, 5 awaken. Wide awake and refreshed.

...death is not an end,
but a birth
into a larger, fuller,
more meaningful life...

CHAPTER 11

The Moment of Death

I have already discussed at length the differences between unconscious dying and conscious dying. By now I trust you have noted the
numerous advantages offered by the latter. In this chapter we will deal
specifically with the exact moment of the transition into spirit known
as death.

The data and theories I present in this chapter come from my experience as a hypnotherapist since 1974. During that time, I have
regressed and progressed over 11,000 individual patients into 33,000
different lifetimes. Furthermore, the work of near-death-experience
researchers (see chapter 2) supports the conclusions I have made and
the paradigms I have created. Lastly, the philosophies of the
Theosophists and Ascended Masters are compatible with the concepts
presented here.

We are all aware that death, like taxes, is unavoidable. The many
cases of NDE illustrate how peaceful this transition is. All pain and discomforts end at the moment of death. The soul has left the body. For
the purpose of this discussion I will describe unconscious dying.

Think about death for a moment. The realization that death is not an end but a birth into a larger, fuller, and more meaningful life is quite beautiful. Death is merely an exchange of an old body for a new one. Death signifies the beginning of a rest and reevaluation period. It is a form of recreation and renewal. It is a transition state, not a state of termination. Death may be hard to explain or to understand, but it is not to be feared. The elimination of the fear of death is but one of the many advantages to conscious dying.

For the time being I would like you to put aside thoughts of Heaven, Hell, and even Purgatory. Put aside religious convictions and open your mind to what I have to say. Of course you don't have to accept this information—all I ask is that you consider it with an open mind.

When we die we are really not dead in the common use of the word. We may be nonfunctional on the earth plane, but we are quite functional on other planes. We exist then on the astral plane, and eventually we will enter the white light and end up on the soul plane (see chapters 3 and 12). Therefore, what we think of as death is really shifting to another plane of existence.

The cells in our body are dying and being replaced constantly as I stated in chapter 1. One of the purposes of the sleep state, at least from a medical point of view, is to re-create the many millions of cells that are killed during each day that we live. We are also replacing lost energy during sleep. Scientists tell us that about every nine months, each and every one of our cells has been replaced at least once.

So, technically, we die every nine months. Our body is completely different than it was one year ago and it will be completely different at this time next year. We obviously don't feel dead, and are able to function quite nicely. The process of cell replacement continues along so smoothly that we are not aware of anything different happening. It is our physical perception that is being fooled into thinking that the body is unchanged from year to year.

In chapter 3, I discussed the cycle of birth and death and briefly described the soul's journey through the white light into the soul plane.

For the purpose of this discussion, we are going to focus on the events following the moment of death.

Quantum physics tells us that our mind creates our reality. This principle is particularly evident at the moment of death. Whatever you think you should experience is exactly what you do perceive. It may be the fires of Hell, or your expectation might manifest itself as angels playing their harps. The presence of religious figures, such as Jesus, Buddha, or Moses, might become a part of your scenario.

Whichever mental movie you create will last only as long as you require to adjust to the astral plane where you also have a body, but a less material one. Your Higher Self and Masters and Guides join you and then karmic reality takes over. These perfect entities will patiently inform you of your transition from the physical plane, even though you may still deny this fact. Your world doesn't seem very different.

Two discrepancies will be noted by your soul at this time. For one thing, you are now totally free of any discomfort you were previously suffering from. Second, you are able to view your own lifeless physical body. This last observation is sometimes quite shocking to your astral body. I should also point out that all of your senses are especially acute at this time—most noticeably your hearing.

Your communication will now be entirely by telepathy. All present can read your every thought, so telling the truth is the rule at this time. There is no hypocrisy on the astral plane. Your nighttime dreams, which are examples of out-of-body experiences, are similar to what your soul encounters now.

The soul always has free will, even on the astral plane. You do not have to enter the white light or even listen to your Higher Self and Masters and Guides. If you choose to ignore everything going on about you and panic, you will be a troubled spirit (ghost) and remain in this state indefinitely.

It is understandable why you might fear the white light, especially since we are discussing unconscious dying. What is real? Your previous prejudices and religious training can come into play now. The white light could be a trick. It could lead you to Hell, couldn't it?

We know that the white light is your only salvation. Your soul will exercise its free will and make its judgment based on many factors. The karmic cycle in general, the environment of the astral plane, the soul's state of mind, and other factors influence this decision process. The amount of time it takes to complete this process can range from a few minutes to a few thousand earth years.

You will note I use the term "earth years." The astral plane does not have the same time concept as we here on the physical plane experience. The space-time continuum becomes even more pronounced as we leave the earth plane. All time is simultaneous and all past, present, and future events can be noted on the astral plane and are, in fact, happening all at once.

Interestingly, there is rarely any form of correlation between a patient's religion and his or her experience of death. In other words, it doesn't seem to matter whether the patient is an agnostic, atheist, Christian, Jew, Hindu, or any other belief; the experiences reported to me are similar.

COMPONENTS OF DEATH

Cross Over

I already mentioned the absence of discomfort at the moment of death. The soul now experiences a floating sensation. This will be accompanied by feelings of quiet and inner peace. There will usually no longer be a sense of fear. The soul feels completely detached from its former physical body.

Patients soon realize that they have a body, but a very different type of body, subject to very different physical laws. This astral body possesses the ability to do many things that the physical body cannot. For example, this astral body can move through walls and doors, and travel thousands of miles in a matter of seconds. Time is not registered at this level; the astral body possesses complete knowledge of the former life and can even read the minds of other people who were involved in that life.

The Silver Cord

The presence of a silver cord is sometimes reported during NDEs. The difference at the moment of death is that this pulsating silver cord stops pulsating and it is now broken. During an NDE the silver cord is attached to the back of the head of the astral body and to the solar plexus region of the physical body on earth. As long as this silver cord is unbroken, the patient's physical body is still alive. Upon death the cord is broken.

Death Sounds

There are several types of noises people hear on the astral plane following their death. Roars, clicks, whistling, musical sounds, and loud ringing noises predominate. Bright colored lights accompany these sounds and this combination is apparently part of the mechanism of changing from the earth to the astral plane. It must be remembered that the soul's frequency vibrational rate is undergoing an alteration at this time too. These special effects occur at a rapid rate.

The Tunnel

A vacuum-like effect is felt by the soul now as it moves through a deep, dark tunnel. This tunnel functions as a type of bridge from the earth plane to the astral plane. It is comparable to a black hole in that it represents a disorientation to the space-time continuum and results in the change from one dimension to the next.

When I regress or progress patients, I usually suggest they imagine themselves entering a tunnel that has a bright white light at the end. I suggest that there is a fork at the end of the tunnel. If the patient takes the right fork he ends up in a past life. A future life would be the destination if the left fork were taken. This technique is very successful, and one of the most commonly used methods of guiding a patient into a past or future life. Whether in a hypnotic state or death, the tunnel clearly seems to represent the passageway to the next level.

The Presence of Others

I have already discussed the fact that the soul is joined by its Masters and Guide, Higher Self, and, occasionally, departed friends and relatives. This happens only after the soul has adjusted to the astral plane. Love dominates now as the soul is filled with feelings of warmth, security, and inner peace. If the soul responds appropriately to this, all fears of death are removed.

The White Light

The white light first makes its appearance at the end of the tunnel I described earlier. This is a blinding, yet peaceful aura of pure white light. Sometimes the soul reports yellow or golden auras, but the light is most commonly described as white.

It is absolutely imperative that the soul enter this white light. There is no other way it can travel to the soul plane. I discussed in chapter 2 that this white light is actually the Higher Self, and that eventually most souls do enter it and continue their travels to the soul plane.

Individual Variations

The experiences of death don't always follow the order I've described. Also, there may be time lags between each step. Some people accept the death state quickly and easily. Others require more time and guidance before they will even accept the idea of death, let alone enter the white light.

Remember, it is your expectations of what the death state is supposed to be that will affect the actual experience. If you expect to be surrounded by haloed angels in white robes playing harps, your Masters and Guides will do their very best to create that scene for you because they know that it will make you feel comfortable. It is only when you are comfortable that these higher entities will inform you about where you are, who they are, and what you are supposed to be doing.

The main point of this chapter is to demonstrate that death is not an experience to fear. Perhaps it is not something to look forward to, but it is not to be feared.

Accounts of death from past-life regressions may not be sufficient evidence for some of you. There have been numerous reports of patients pronounced clinically dead (NDE) (see chapter 2) who eventually survived. When asked of their experiences, they have reported startlingly similar observations to those presented here. Yet, these people experiencing near-death have usually never heard of past-life regression.

If people from different religious backgrounds who are regressed, and people who have clinically died and returned to life all report similar experiences, the correspondences between these descriptions are more than coincidental. Yet, in the final analysis, you must form your own opinions. Death is an experience you will face many times. It is up to you to interpret this concept to fit your own particular beliefs. It is also your responsibility to make this transition a conscious dying rather than an unconscious death.

My intention is to remove much of the misconception about the experience, so that when the time comes for you to die, your experience will be as peaceful and serene as possible. This is even more important when you practice the art of conscious dying.

At the moment of death most souls show little interest in their former body. They appear to want to get on to the spiritual world, and the Higher Self is always present advising the soul at this time. Souls that do hover around the body are more common among children who have died. Another reason for this unwillingness to depart, especially for adults, is a yearning to comfort loved ones left behind on the physical plane.

An Eastern view of the moment of death and the bardo states will be described in chapter 19 as I rigorously discuss the *Tibetan Book of the Dead*.[1] For our purposes let us say that the death process is more like snow melting. Boundaries between the physical and nonphysical world become less defined. It is more like a withdrawal of the soul from one level of consciousness to another. There is no time as we know it in the

---

1   Evans-Wentz, 1960.

nonphysical world. All time is simultaneous. The new physics refers to this as space-time (Appendices A and B of *The Search for Grace*[2] discuss this in greater detail. There is also a discussion of the time concept in *Soul Healing*[3]).

An expansion beyond what we are accustomed to calling the physical plane is noteworthy during the dying process. The soul is being transferred from a very physical body to a less material one, and often is unaware that a change has taken place. Thus, death may be described as a sense of expanding beyond oneself, of dissolving out of form, and of melting into the undifferentiated. Once this process begins, unless the Higher Self or one's Masters and Guides instruct the soul to return to the physical body, it is irreversible.

The white light is the most significant awareness the soul has at this time. The soul may be freed of pain and discomfort, but the brilliance of this light supersedes all awareness. The amount of time this process takes depends on the spiritual evolution of the soul and its willingness to accept this transition. All of this is, of course, facilitated by conscious dying.

CONSCIOUS DYING AND THE MOMENT OF DEATH

When one is proficient in conscious dying my previous descriptions will be somewhat inaccurate. The transition now will be a far more peaceful and spiritual one. This moment should be filled with peace and quiet, along with compassion and love from all present. It ideally should take place in the home, as I discussed in chapter 4.

Conscious dying will also result in the soul's awareness of various ESP abilities, such as telepathy, clairvoyance, telekinesis, etc. Transcendence is used to refer to this initial step in liberation of the soul. An awareness of the nonphysical world and an acceptance of the inability to return to the physical world will also be evident at this time.

---

2   Dr. Bruce Goldberg. *The Search for Grace* (St. Paul, MN: Llewellyn Publications, 1997). Previously published by In Print Publishing, Sedona, AZ.

3   Goldberg, 1996.

This new nonphysical world is one of pure consciousness and of total freedom. It is quite a different bardo than one experiences as a result of unconscious dying. The transitee who has died consciously is not bound to any world. This soul is liberated.

An interesting medical fact about the moment of death is that man is one of the few animals to open his eyes at the moment of death. Not only do we open them, but we open them wider. Is this caused by the brilliant white light?

Feelings of profound peace dominate the soul once the transition is made. All senses that we use on the physical plane operate in the non-physical world. The sense of hearing is especially acute and the soul can listen to conversations and other sounds from the physical plane it just left.

Remember, the soul that has consciously died is likely to have ended its cycle of birth and death. It is in a state of bliss. Other names for this level of pure consciousness are:

Nirvana (Buddhism)

Anuttara-Samyak-Sambodhi (Buddhism)

Nirvikalpa Samadhi (Yoga)

Kaivalya (Yoga)

Moksha (Hinduism)

The Absolute *Tao* (Laotse)

Satori (Zen)

Kensho-godo (Zen)

Fana (Sufi)

Kingdom of Heaven; Perfection (Jesus)

Clear Light (Tibetan)

A feeling of oneness with one's own Higher Self and the universe is a very important component of this bliss. No longer are we bound by the illusions created by the mind. No longer are we contaminated by the negative forces and attitudes that so dominate the physical plane. We are free.

As dying occurs, the soul begins to release all of its backlogged desires, feelings, fears, and negative tendencies. There is no need for this baggage in the nonphysical world occupied by your Higher Self, Masters and Guides, and departed loved ones who only mean you well.

Summarizing the Moment of Death

- There is a brilliance emanating from a white light.

- There is no pain.

- Peace and love are noted immediately.

- The soul emerges and is transformed to be with its Higher and perfect Self.

- The silver cord is severed.

- Telepathy and other ESP are exhibited.

- Unusual sounds are heard.

- The tunnel experience begins.

- The presence of other loving entities is felt.

- There is total awareness of the physical world left behind and the nonphysical one just entered.

If, by reading this chapter, you have shed even one aspect of your fear of death, my efforts have been worthwhile.

...we can custom design
our future lives
as well as the future
of our current lifetime

CHAPTER 12

Choosing Your Next Life

To summarize the actual transition the soul makes in unconscious dying: from the moment of death the entity is placed in a very precarious position. This is a transition or adjustment period. We must first be made aware of the fact that we have died. This is accomplished by helpful guidance from highly evolved entities such as our Higher Self and Masters and Guides. These Masters and Guides have completed their karmic cycles many centuries ago. Their main purpose now is to help us adjust to the fact that we have died, and to lead us to the white light that will take us to the soul plane, where we will evaluate our previous life and choose our next.

At this time, we may also see and communicate by telepathy with friends or relatives who have previously died. These entities will also try to persuade us to enter the white light. If you don't enter the white light you will remain on the astral plane as a troubled spirit. Some recently departed entities will find comfort in the last surroundings they inhabited on the earth plane. Thus, they will frequent, in spirit, their house or apartment. Some of their family may be made aware of their presence and could interpret this as a ghost haunting their house. Indeed, many cases of haunted houses can be explained in this fashion. Of course, during this transition your Higher Self is continually present and will attempt to discourage this behavior. You, as a soul, still have free will to ignore this advice.

THE SOUL PLANE

Eventually, you will enter the white light and your destination will be the soul plane. Upon arriving at the soul plane, you will be greeted by special guides who are assigned specifically to you for the purpose of orientation. Your guides will spend as much time as necessary to explain the nature of reality and discuss your present purpose on this plane. You will be shown detailed events from your last life and how they fit into your karmic patterns. Also, you will be shown scenes from past and future lives, and be requested to study these events in detail. You are given a tremendous amount of help and advice by your Masters and Guides and Higher Self in these all-important decisions. However, it is always your responsibility to make the choice concerning your next life. The soul always has free will. This is part of your empowerment.

It must be remembered at this time that if you practice conscious dying techniques properly, the need to reincarnate on the lower planes does not exist, but just as Buddha decided to not ascend and remain as a Master, you may also choose to stay around for a while to assist other less-evolved souls. Even when that is not your goal, your soul's energy level may have been too low to ascend after just one conscious dying experience. You must live again and consciously die at least one more time to remove yourself from the cycle of birth and death.

Astrology plays a major role in deciding a time period for your next life. The exact time, place, and date of birth will be very important. If you have artistic lessons to learn and sensitivity is to be experienced, then coming back as a Pisces would be indicated. Learning lessons as an executive or leader might dictate coming back as a

Scorpio, Capricorn, or Leo. Of course, your other planetary influences such as the Moon, Ascendant, Mars, Mercury, Venus, etc., must also be carefully selected.

In addition to astrology, "subcycles" must also be taken into consideration before any decision concerning the overall karmic cycle can be made. Within our karmic cycles, these smaller sub-cycles, such as certain emotional, intellectual, creative, and physical tasks, when completed, finish a certain phase within the total karmic cycle. Some parapsychologists say that every twelve lives make up a sub-cycle. These twelve lives correspond to the zodiac signs in astrology. Theoretically, we choose a different astrological sign in each of these twelve lives to complete the cycle.

There is something called a "karmic chart" which can be constructed from your birth date, time, and place. This is quite different from a regular astrological or natal chart in that it specifies what your sub-cycle is and can give you great insight into your overall karmic cycle. This is also referred to as a Vedic chart.

On the soul plane, you will also be choosing your parents, brothers, sisters, and other family members, as well as planning all the major events in your life. These events must take into consideration the karmic cycle of these other people.

The actual descriptions I have received from my patients about the soul plane range from domed facilities with several others reviewing the lives of the soul, to Tibetan mountain tops, and even different planets. Whatever your soul creates as this environment it apparently will receive.

Not only must you be fully aware of your own karmic cycle, but you must at least be familiar with the karmic cycles of the many significant people that you will come into contact with in your new life. Whether you will be rich or poor, an only child or a member of a large family, black or white, weak or strong, will all depend on a very complicated selection process that your past-life history will decide. Your Akashic records have all of this information and they will be your constant reference on the soul plane.

Akashic Records

These Akashic records, as I previously pointed out, are reportedly kept on the causal plane, but we do have access to them on the soul plane. They represent a file on the soul's growth and development throughout its many lives. They contain what the soul has learned and not learned. Thus, the soul's progression through its karmic cycle is what the Akashic records will show. By using these records we have intimate knowledge of what we have done and what we have to do. This is a most valuable aid.

For example, because of past karmic debts, in your next life you might need to stress the intellect. The emotional side of living would be underplayed so that the intellect could be developed to its maximum potential. Or the opposite situation might present itself. Your physical status is also important. A handicap, although it seems an obvious disadvantage in your new life, gives you the opportunity to learn certain lessons that would be difficult to learn if no such defect existed.

Masters and Guides

We are aided in making these decisions by our Masters and Guides. These highly evolved entities have completed their karmic cycles and their purpose is simply to help and advise us as to our next lives. We may have known these entities in past lives. They do not moralize or pass judgment. They simply counsel us and try to help us the best they can. The individual soul always has free will to ignore their advice. Many of our decisions are poorly made for this very reason. These Masters and Guides also receive advice from even higher entities with higher vibrational rates in the seven higher planes. These much more advanced entities receive their advice from even more evolved sources, the ultimate authority being God. The final result is, of course, excellent guidance. When we listen to these guides, we make better decisions and work out our karmic cycles faster and with much less trauma.

The outline of the process of moving from the death experience to the soul plane will now be described in greater detail. The most comprehensive book published to date on the details of this between-lives state is Michael Newton's *Journey of Souls*.[1] In this book Michael describes a most complex mechanism for this interlife process.

The soul is greeted at the soul plane by "welcoming entities" who may not be part of this soul's learning team in this new dimension. The more spiritually evolved souls do not require this initiation to the soul plane. The trip to the soul plane is often described as being pulled along an energy wave as if by a magnet. The soul can generate some of this electricity itself.

Next in line is a "shower of healing" which is a form of energy bath that cleanses the soul of the difficulties from its previous life. A debriefing is given only to younger souls by their guide before they are transferred to a central port that is divided into clusters.

A cluster is made up of from five to twenty souls who are initially assigned to it and who return to this same group after each incarnation. The souls do not wander about but stay huddled together. It is during this time that the souls are distributed according to their level of spiritual evolvement and become bonded as they converse about their recent lifetime. Guides are ever present and offer advice and counsel.

In each cluster souls will find that their colleagues represent approximately the same level of growth. This "Inner Cycle" is very close in its communication between the member souls. There is, however, little contact with other clusters and almost no interaction with less advanced souls.

Newton lists six levels of souls, each possessing a different color in their aura. Level I souls are termed beginner and have a white hue. Level IIs are called lower intermediate and have reddish shades to their white aura. It is in Level III (intermediate) that the hue becomes a solid yellow. Level IV is upper intermediate and is a dark yellow with traces of blue aura. It has the status of a junior guide. Level V is an advanced soul with a light blue showing traces of purple in its aura. This is the level of a senior guide. Finally, in Level VI (a highly advanced soul) we find a dark blue to purple aura; this is also a master guide.

---

1 Michael Newton, *Journey of Souls* (St. Paul, MN: Llewellyn Publications, 1994), excerpt used with permission.

Dr. Newton's research reveals that the percentage of each level he sees are: Level I: 42%; Level II: 31%, Level III: 17%; Level IV: 9%; Level V: 1%. He never sees Level VI souls, nor would I expect that such an advanced soul would require his services. Thus, nearly three quarters of all souls inhabiting human bodies on earth today are immature souls.

The basic principles (on pages 105–106 of his book) and soul group assignment he reports are:

- Regardless of the relative time of creation after their novice status is completed, all beginner souls are assigned to a new group of souls at their own level of understanding.

- Once a new soul support group is formed, no new members are added in the future.

- There appears to be a systematic procedure for homogeneous groupings of souls selected by cognitive awareness who display similar characteristics of ego-identity.

- Irrespective of size, cluster groups do not directly intermix with each other's energy, but souls can communicate with one another across primary and secondary group boundaries.

- Primary clusters may split into smaller sub-groups for study, but are not separated from the integrated whole within a single cluster of souls.

- Rates of learning vary among peer group members. Certain souls will advance faster than others in a cluster group. Their physical energy leaves the cluster when they attain an intermediate level of development. These souls are then loosely formed into an "independent studies" work group with their old guides monitoring them, usually under one master guide. Thus, a new pod of entities graduating into Level III could be brought together from many clusters within one or more secondary groups.

- Although group size diminishes as souls advance, the intimate contact between peer group members is never lost.

- Spiritual guides have a wide variety of teaching methods and instructional personifications depending on group composition.

These clusters appear to lack the disrespect, suspicion, hatred, and jealousies that we find on earth. There are no power struggles, secrets, or attempts at manipulation. The soul is given more responsibilities as it advances in level. During Levels III and IV, for example, souls are assigned younger souls as students.

After much counsel with their guides in planning a new life, the soul enters the "Ring of Destiny" where it reviews various options for its future incarnation. Only after this option is selected is a new body chosen. Lastly, the soul attends a "recognition class" to assist in recognizing and properly utilizing opportunities in the new life. The trip to a new body is considerably faster than the reverse.

All of Newton's descriptions assume an unconscious death and rebirth. Since the purpose of this book is conscious dying and rebirth (if necessary), let us see how the rebirth process differs.

CONSCIOUS REBIRTH

The process of conscious rebirth is the same as that of conscious dying, but in opposite directions. Please refer back to Figure 1 (page 10) and note how the soul moves from the soul plane, avoiding the karmic cycle and into the physical body. The Higher Self is acting as a guide throughout this process. The connection or awareness of the soul to the Higher Self is kept intact at this time.

There is no fear of what the future body will hold in conscious rebirth. There is no misunderstanding of the laws of the universe. There is no repression of previous lives or experiences on the soul plane.

The soul is fully aware that it chose the newborn and the framework of its new lifetime for spiritual growth. The subconscious knows it selected its parents, friends, occupation, physical limitations, future mate, and children long before this sojourn began.

Thus, conscious dying leads to conscious rebirth. Unconscious dying can only lead to unconscious rebirth. If the soul is experiencing conscious rebirth, the following will characterize its initial experiences in the newborn:

- An awareness and knowledge of one's own true karmic purpose.

- An establishment of contact with our Higher Self.

- An awareness of God.

- An awareness of our inherent immortality.

- The elimination of the fear of rebirth.

- Contact with Masters and Guides and departed loved ones.

- Empowerment as expressed by control over our destiny. We can custom design our future lives as well as the future of our current lifetime. At last we can be "master of our fate and captain of our soul."

- The elimination of the need to be born again by karmic necessity.

You will note that these elements are also exhibited in conscious dying.

CHOOSING A NEW BODY

This is a very complicated process and group karmic considerations must be met. That is, you have to consider the karmic cycle of dozens of other entities before you can finalize your plans. These other entities must agree with your plans because they also have free will. This veto power can cause untold delays in the final framework of your and their next lives.

There can even be competition for certain bodies. Let's assume that you have completed your design of the basic framework for your next life. Now you must choose a newborn to enter. But let's say that another entity desires this same newborn for his or her karmic cycle and gets the right to inhabit it. You still have a karmic cycle to work out with the parents and other members of that newborn's family. You will now have to find another suitable newborn and devise a way to relate karmically to the parents and other family members of the newborn you were prevented from entering. We don't know exactly how the order on the waiting list for bodies is decided. It is probably based on a priority system, giving first priority to those souls with the most important karmic lessons to learn.

Once you have carefully chosen your next body and designed the basic framework of your next life, you are ready for the soul's entrance into the newborn. During the course of the pregnancy, each soul may visit its future body. Indeed, many souls actually enter the developing fetus, and this is why many people have prenatal memories that can be tapped through the use of hypnosis.

One reason that the soul can come and go as it pleases at this time is because the fetus' nervous system has not yet fully developed. There are openings in the skull (cranium) called "fontanelles" which allow the soul or subconscious to enter or leave the body. These openings will not close until the child is about two and one-half years old. This helps explain the psychic nature of children. The work of Professor Ian Stevenson of the University of Virginia shows that children are most likely to exhibit spontaneous past life regressions between the ages of two and one-half and five.

The soul or subconscious actually enters the body of the newborn within twenty-four hours before or after the birth of the child. Many times during our childhood the soul will leave the body. This will occur during the waking hours as well as at night as the entity sleeps. All throughout our life the soul will leave the body during our sleep state, because it is during this sleep state that our Masters and Guides and Higher Self can continue teaching and advising us on our earthly progress. Earlier I pointed out that all dreams are examples of out-of-body experiences. We are never really without the benefit of our guides, and the process of learning that began in between our lives never really ends.

CHAPTER 12

OTHER DECISIONS ON THE SOUL PLANE

Much counsel is given to an entity on the soul plane. However, even with all this advice and plenty of time to make these decisions, some people choose to reincarnate before they are advised to. This is unfortunate because the necessary planning has not occurred. Instead of saving time, much time will be wasted and many errors will be made.

Relationships represent important decisions on the soul plane. Telepathic communication between you and the other entities involved will establish the details of who you will relate with and how in your next life. Your son in this life may be your father in your next life. Your wife or husband may be your brother or employer or parent.

Soul mates, or people with whom you have had very significant love relationships over many lifetimes, will be handled carefully. These soul mates represent the culmination of many lifetimes of being together and of sharing the most valuable emotion of all. You will not, however, be with your soul mates in every life. For a more detailed discussion of the different types of soul mates, I refer you to my book *Soul Healing*.[2]

Remember that during conscious rebirth the soul has all memories of its former lives and its transition is far less difficult than that of unconscious rebirth.

There is sound medical evidence to show that the developing fetus can respond to the earth plane prior to its actual birth. Thomas Verney, M.D., in his book *The Secret Life of the Unborn Child*, states, "The fetus can see, hear, experience, taste and, on a primitive level, even learn in utero....Most importantly, he can feel—not with an adult's sophistication, but feel nonetheless."[3]

Dr. Verney's research shows that the fetus reacts to the mother's feelings and thoughts, as well as music. It is most likely the neurohormonal connection between the mother and the fetus that is responsible

---

2   Goldberg, 1996.

3   Thomas Verney (with John Kelly), *The Secret Life of the Unborn Child* (New York: Summit Books, 1981), p. 12.

for this. The fetus' health is affected by the mother's emotional states. This carries on into that of the newborn.

The mechanics of a typical hospital's delivery system for the newborn does leave a lot to be desired. The following recommendations will facilitate and support the process of conscious rebirth.

1. The elimination of spinal shock to the newborn, when it is held upside down following delivery. A more gentle orientation to the earth plane is indicated.

2. The reduction, if not elimination, of loud noises in the delivery room. Such sounds from instruments and doctors and nurses should be kept to a minimal volume to avoid shocking the newborn.

3. The elimination of the separation of the child from its mother upon delivery. A far better solution is to immediately place the newborn with its mother.

4. The elimination of shock to the newborn's eyes by dimming the lights in the delivery room. This will allow the baby's eyes to become accustomed to the light as the brightness is increased gradually.

5. The elimination of respiratory shock to the newborn by waiting a few minutes longer before cutting the umbilical cord. This reduces the excessive heat being transmitted to the newborn's lungs due to sudden oxidation.

"I am now an unreasonably
happy person …
thanks to conscious dying
and your guidance"

CHAPTER 13

A Mother's Conscious Dying with Her Son

Janine's case is a most unusual example of conscious dying. Her history represented one victimization after another. In her early twen-
ties, she married a physically and psychologically abusive man named
Steve. They had one son, Michael. During this eight-year union,
Janine's grandmother died and left her nearly one hundred thousand
dollars as an inheritance.

This was Janine's first personal experience with death. She loved
her grandmother and grieved for her for several years. Steve took nearly seventy thousand dollars from Janine before he finally divorced her.

This resulted in Janine becoming severely depressed. She always
exhibited needy tendencies, but now she was more co-dependent than
ever. When Vance came into her life, Janine was at her lowest level of
misery. She could barely take care of her and Michael's needs as she
taught at a private school and did not earn much money. One promise
she had made herself was never to use the remainder of her inheritance
to live on until she retired from working.

She began dating Vance, but was not in love with him per se. This was a relationship of convenience on both ends. Vance was a drifter with no career and even less desire to work. Janine needed someone to cling to, other than her son Michael.

Vance, like Steve, was several years younger than Janine. This was one of her vulnerabilities. They were married after only a few months of dating. Vance immediately moved in with Janine and Michael and simply lived off Janine's salary. She did not inform Vance of her inheritance, as she was already scarred from her experience with her ex-husband, but one New Year's Eve, Vance got Janine very drunk and she told him about her nest egg. Vance then began to look for ways to "invest" this money. Janine would have no part of this until Vance threatened to leave her if she refused to trust him with her money.

Janine acquiesced and turned over the account to Vance. Some months later, Janine came home to an empty apartment. Vance had left her, taking most of their furniture and all of her remaining inheritance.

This left Janine broke, depressed, and lonely. She had to borrow money to rent furniture so that her son wouldn't have to sleep on the floor. To compensate for her many problems, Janine developed compulsive spending habits. She would splurge and spend the few extra dollars she saved. In addition, she had insomnia that coincided with her growing financial problems, and a long history of various allergies.

She was also a frustrated musician. She played the guitar and wanted to do so professionally. Michael represented the only joy in her life. Her job was boring and unfulfilling. She most certainly was not prepared for what was about to happen.

Her physician recommended a hysterectomy to treat a long-standing medical problem. Janine reluctantly agreed to this surgery. She nearly died during the operation. In fact, she had a classic near-death experience (NDE).

As it turned out, this NDE became a turning point in her life. This second experience with death resulted in tremendous spiritual growth for her. Janine's mood problems all but disappeared. She seemed to develop a new lease on life. No longer was she depressed.

Many things had not changed. She still hated her job, still had no money, and no prospects as a musician. Her allergies also remained unaffected by this experience. Janine kept away from men and still had insomnia. At least she was not depressed.

It was at this time that she just "happened" to come across my first book, *Past Lives—Future Lives*,[1] in her local bookstore. She called me to set up appointments for herself and her son.

They both came to my Los Angeles office in 1989. Michael was now nine years old and a good hypnotic patient. I conducted past life regression and future life progression on both of them. Cleansing techniques were done, at first separately, and then together on Janine and Michael.

It is admittedly most uncommon to train a nine-year old in conscious dying techniques. Janine had insisted I do this with him as well as with her. My explanation of the theory and procedure had to be considerably simplified for Michael. I felt he had some idea what we were doing but his mother promised to further educate him as he grew older.

When I asked her why she felt it was so important for me to train Michael at this stage of his life in conscious dying, she stated that the instructions to have Michael trained in conscious dying came to her in a dream. This dream occurred shortly after her NDE, suggesting that it was more likely a Higher Self contact.

Janine became very emotional during her sessions. She responded with overwhelming joy during the cleansings. This represented quite a welcome change from the boring and unfulfilling teaching job she was to go back to upon returning from Los Angeles. She and Michael looked forward to using the self-hypnosis tapes I made for them.

The next contact I had with her was three years later. A few months before Michael (then twelve years old) had gone camping with his best friend's family and drowned in a boating accident. Janine was shocked at first but quickly settled down and continued with her conscious dying techniques. Her bereavement was short (about three

---

1   Goldberg, 1988.

weeks) and she reported another unusual ability. It seemed that on several occasions she felt a strange "tingly feeling" in her legs. This would be followed by a telepathic communication from Michael's soul.

From the very first time it happened, Janine felt comfortable with this phenomenon. Michael told her that he was safe and with his angel (he always referred to his Higher Self as his angel). He said that she should not worry about him and that one day she will be with her angel.

I asked her how she felt about this and she informed me that she was at peace with her life. Janine fully accepted Michael's death and felt that he died consciously. She also feels confident that she will be able to die consciously when it is her time.

Her life also showed remarkable progress since I last saw them. She no longer has allergies. Compulsive spending is long since gone, as are her insomnia and headaches. She quit her job and obtained a more interesting and better-paying position with a large accounting firm. In addition, she met a good man and has been in a very fulfilling relationship for over a year.

Lastly, she now plays in a rock band on weekends and occasionally in a blues band. She appears to be in complete control of her life.

She wrote me a very nice letter and in it she stated, "My heart is overwhelmed with love and understanding for people, animals, and things. I am now officially an unreasonably happy person thanks to conscious dying and your guidance."

Not only am I happy for her growth, but Janine's case comes almost as close as you can get to documenting the theoretical basis for conscious dying: that a soul actually does come back, avoiding the disorienting forces of the karmic cycle (see Figure 1, page 10). In chapter 15 I will present a rather impressive example of a documented case of conscious dying.

...the cleansing experience
...results in
a state of mind
of peace and tranquility

CHAPTER 14

A Conscious Dying in a Hospital

S everal years ago, I received an emergency call from a man concerning his wife. Norm had just admitted his wife Rose to Johns Hopkins Hospital for a severe pulmonary (lung) disorder. It seemed that Rose had use of only 20 percent of her lungs and the situation was medically critical.

Rose read my first book, *Past Lives—Future Lives*[1] and wanted to experience a future life progression. She knew her time on the earth plane was about to expire. Several specialists examined her and were unanimous in their opinion of her condition. Rose did not have long to live.

Rose instructed her husband, Norm, to arrange for me to come to her hospital room to conduct hypnotherapy with her. Since Rose knew she was about to die, she wanted to be assured that she would live again in a new body at some future date.

Norm didn't share Rose's belief in reincarnation. He was aware of my reputation and respected me, but simply didn't think his wife or anyone else was capable of "coming back."

---

1   Goldberg, 1988.

Since I have a hospital residency training as part of my post-graduate dental education, I did have hospital privileges with Johns Hopkins and arranged to meet with her. You can imagine the attitude of some of the more conventional physicians at this institution when I arrived.

My initial interview with Rose revealed several things. First, Rose was very depressed. She had had an unfulfilling life and was ill for most of it. Her relationship with Norm was far from ideal. Although Rose came from a wealthy family, this did not assure her happiness.

The second factor I observed was a diametrically opposite attitude between her physician and the nurses. Where the nurses were totally supportive of my work, Rose's lung specialist objected to my very presence. His objections were based solely on the fact that he did not believe in reincarnation and felt my presence would somehow embarrass him.

Fortunately, the hospital did not share his antagonism and allowed me to work with Rose. I was briefed by her specialist, who informed me that Rose had at most four weeks to live. Norm and Rose were told this and the prognosis did not help Rose's depressed state.

I liked Rose from the moment I met her. She was truly motivated to work with me. As a lifelong believer in reincarnation (this is not necessary for conscious dying to be effective), Rose was well read and an excellent hypnotic patient.

Rose did ask me if I would allow several of her nurses to witness her therapy. Naturally, I had no objection to this. My sessions were done with Norm and between three and six nurses present.

I did take a brief history from Rose and discovered that she did not lead a happy life. As a woman in her sixties with no children and only Norm at her side, she appeared almost numb. She did not love Norm and never had. All through her life, Rose was depressed and victimized by a long string of psychosomatic illnesses. She had respiratory (breathing) problems through most of her life. Looking at her lack of emotional expression, I could see why she was ready to die.

Norm informed me of Rose's unhappy life and felt somewhat guilty about his role in it. He really tried to make her happy but he had many problems of his own.

The nurses were helpful to me in providing additional background to Rose's state of mind since she was admitted, in addition to the medications she was taking. Rose was continually monitored by various machines, so it was not easy to move around in her room.

My initial session with her ended with a lengthy hypnotic trance and a superconscious mind scan of several of her past lives. I then initiated a cleansing to train her to raise the frequency vibrational rate of her subconscious (soul). Finally a future life progression was conducted.

During Rose's future life, in the middle of the twenty-first century, she saw herself as a happy young woman involved with charitable institutions. She helped many people far less fortunate than herself. In addition, she had a husband and two children and was very happy.

Up to this time Rose expressed no emotions. She was merely depressed and could hardly speak. Now she cried with joy and began to act in an animated fashion. This welcome change shocked Norm and the nurses, who were not accustomed to seeing Rose act this way.

At the end of this long session I told Rose and Norm that I would return the following day and the rest of the week would be spent training Rose in the art of conscious dying.

They readily agreed and Rose acted like a child with a new toy. I gave her some self-hypnosis tapes to play to assist her orientation of my techniques. Each day I spent at Johns Hopkins was more rewarding than the day before. Rose responded quite well and Norm appeared to change his attitude to what I was doing.

The hospital spread the word quickly about my work with Rose. Each day I saw different nurses and interns who wanted to witness this therapy for themselves. Rose now could laugh and cry. She still had problems speaking and breathing, but this was most definitely a different person.

Although the staff asked a lot of questions about the theoretical foundation for what I was doing, my time had to be spent clinically attending to Rose. They were ever considerate and patiently waited until I took a break in the clinical procedures before questioning me.

I felt as though I was conducting a workshop, spending every coffee break and lunch break discussing the details and theoretical basis of karma, reincarnation, quantum physics, and conscious dying.

As the end of each week and the completion of my therapy with Rose approached, Norm appeared to change his lifelong opinion about reincarnation. He could not believe the complete change in Rose's demeanor. For the first time since he had known her, Rose appeared to be at peace. The expression "at peace" was repeated to me by the nurses and Rose herself several times. This is one of the many benefits of conscious dying. The cleansing experienced by the patient without exception results in a state of mind of peace and tranquility.

Just before I left the hospital for the last time, I spoke to Rose about all that we had accomplished. This was not just a summary of our treatment or a wrap-up session. I explained that she very soon would have the opportunity to apply these techniques. She understood me and asked some very pertinent questions.

The last words Rose said to me were "God bless you and your work." Two weeks later Norm called to let me know that Rose died. He was with her up to the very end. Just before she died she was smiling and said to him, "The doctor was right, I am ready."

CHAPTER 15

A Documented Case of Conscious Dying

When I first began my work with past life regression in 1974, critics would always say that you cannot prove reincarnation. I agree, but you can present suggestive evidence establishing the hypothesis that the soul lives on in other physical bodies. The only way to do that is to check out and corroborate the data given by the patient during a regression. This has been done many thousands of times by various researchers.

However, my second book, *The Search for Grace*,[1] describes a case of reincarnation that was fully validated by an independent researcher hired by CBS television. This case, based on a regression in 1988, was dramatized in the television movie "Search for Grace" starring Lisa Hartman and Ken Wahl, which first aired on May 17, 1994. Most significant about the documentation was that two facts the patient told me in trance did not check out with newspaper records of the time (1927).

---

1   Goldberg, 1994 and 1997.

CHAPTER 15

In regression she told me that she was thirty-two years old when she died and that her son's name was Cliff. Newspaper reports stated that Grace Doze was thirty years old and referred to her son as Chester, Jr.

A subsequent search for Grace Doze's birth certificate revealed that my patient was correct and the Buffalo newspaper reporters had made minor errors. Since New York is a closed state and political permission (along with a written request filed with the state) is required to obtain these records, it would have been impossible for my patient to have known the true facts prior to 1992 when the research was done. (I had regressed the patient [Ivy] in 1988.) This fact was verified when a representative from the department of public records was interviewed on a local radio station in Buffalo the day the television movie aired. I was also interviewed on the same show.

The reason I discuss this case here is to show the potential problems involved with documentation. It is difficult enough to corroborate a past life. How can one possibly document a case of conscious dying?

Since the patient leaves the earth plane when they consciously die, all communication with me is terminated. The following case, I believe, illustrates not only the benefits of conscious dying, but also gives highly suggestive evidence of a documented case of this experience.

In 1979 a sixty-four-year-old woman came to my office. Edna was dying of cancer and had only a few months to live. When I interviewed her I observed a depressed and lonely woman more afraid of living than of dying.

Edna was a widow and had one son who had died as a teenager many years before in a car accident. She had few friends and felt abandoned by her family. Although she was depressed she was not suicidal. She did not look forward to the next day but was not afraid to die.

Edna long ago had abandoned her belief in God. Her life was so stressful and characterized by so many losses that she believed in nothing. The idea of reincarnation was attractive to her philosophically, but she just was not sure what happened after she died.

The only joy she had in life was playing the piano. Since she was a child she had played classical music on this instrument, but now, due

130

to arthritis and her generally weakened medical condition, this had become impossible. She could no longer play the piano.

Edna's life was one tragedy and loss after another. She was always indecisive, even as a child. Her family nicknamed her "Iffy" to reflect this personality trait of saying, "If only I had done this..."

When I worked with her, several past-life regressions were conducted at her request. She reported several traumatic and unhappy previous lifetimes. Her indecisiveness was exhibited in most of these lives. Interestingly enough, one somewhat positive lifetime was characterized by her playing the piano as a school teacher in the 1800s.

These regressions helped Edna deal with the idea of the immortality of her soul. She was not interested in perceiving a future lifetime, but several conscious dying sessions were conducted. During these cleansings she referred to her spirit guide as Shamani.

Edna appeared much less depressed when I completed her training. She appeared ready to accept and deal with her pending transition, and to apply her conscious dying techniques. Her neighbor always brought Edna to my office and further reinforced my observations.

I will always remember our last conversation. Just before leaving my office for the last time she took my hand and said, "we will meet again." Although that is not unusual to hear from a patient, it is the first time someone with just a few months to live said that to me. Two months later Edna's neighbor informed me that Edna died. The death was reportedly a peaceful one as Edna died with a smile on her face.

In 1988 a couple from the Midwest called my office and made an appointment for their seven-year-old daughter, Paula. This couple was very conventional and had no belief in reincarnation.

Paula's mother saw me conduct a past life regression on the *Phil Donahue Show* and expressed concern about Paula's mental state. She felt I was the perfect therapist for her daughter.

When they arrived at my office, I obtained a detailed history of Paula's "problem." Ever since she began speaking, Paula made several references to her lost family. She talked about her son and husband and how difficult it was to be an old lady living alone. Paula also showed a natural talent and interest in playing the piano. She especially liked playing classical music. This hobby pleased her parents, but it was her earlier behavior that concerned them.

Paula's parents felt that she was "possessed" by some evil spirit and requested that I exorcise this demon out of her. I work with many children in my practice. Paula's attitude and mannerisms were those of a bright, creative, communicative, and happy child. Her parents' concerns were well meaning but my interpretation of Paula's behavior was that she was expressing the mannerisms of her last life.

Paula was in second grade and a model student. She had playmates, but preferred the company of adults, especially her grandparents.

Paula asked if I would mind calling her by her nickname. I said, "of course not," and asked her what that name was. I was literally shocked when she said "Iffy." Her parents confirmed that Paula liked to be called Iffy but they just could not adopt it as her nickname.

Both parents were present when I regressed Paula to her last life. She related to me the story of Edna. Several facts were easily confirmed by my records, and when I conducted this past life regression I had Edna's chart on my desk for reference.

During a superconscious mind tap Paula again shocked me. She spoke of the soul plane and of her guide. She then said, "Shamani says hi." This was the name Edna used to describe her Higher Self.

Paula was born in 1981, just two years after Edna died. Paula could barely read and never read books on reincarnation. Her parents did not believe in past lives, and had absolutely no incentive to have their daughter lie to me. In addition, they could not possibly have known Edna, who had few friends and lived over 1,500 miles away.

There is no logical or conventional explanation for this case. Apparently Edna had to reincarnate but she chose a life in which she is happy and well adjusted. Edna can again play the piano. Since she was consciously reborn she has memories of her past lives.

Welcome back, Edna. Yes, we did meet again and thank you from the depths of my soul for your documented case of conscious dying and conscious rebirth.

...the closer you get
to your transition,
the more you understand
how to live

CHAPTER 16

Your Own Transition

This chapter is written for those suffering from a terminal illness who are about to make the transition into the "other side." Your "terminal illness" may be simply old age. Whatever your particular situation is, this section is given as a guideline to make this metamorphosis a peaceful transition. I am assuming that you have decided to make this transition at home.

The dying patient is always vulnerable to anxiety. I have already described the stages of dying in chapter 8. Please reread that chapter to fully understand what is occurring in your life emotionally.

My perspective is from the energy level, but that does not mean I am insensitive to the emotional turmoil you are experiencing at this time. Your entire world may trigger anxiety at any moment. Every person, event, and communication you experience reminds you that you are dying. Your natural response is to become angry or depressed.

Frustration also sets in. Just as you are assimilating the world around you, a world you will shortly leave, something reminds you of your impending death. Even the word death itself sound so harsh and impersonal. This is one reason why I call this a peaceful transition. The term "death" is, as I have explained throughout this book, inaccurate.

I hope by now that you have adopted a belief system embracing the immortality of the soul. It is not necessary to share that metaphysical concept, but it does make the certainty of this transition easier to take. You are the final judge on this point.

You will find at this time that you have a tendency to prioritize what is important for you to do and who you want to see. Don't be surprised to discover what I refer to as the "transition irony." This simply states that the closer you get to your transition, the more you understand how to live. Think of this time as a rehearsal for a play. The last three months of your physical life require all the faith, knowledge, and support acquired over your entire incarnation to effect your absolutely best performance, conscious dying.

The philosophy of living day by day comes into play here. Plan your day every morning with the goals you most desire to accomplish. This schedule should be uncluttered and structured so that there will be events that offer fulfilling rewards. These may involve accomplishing small but important tasks, or the sharing of intimacies with loved ones.

One goal that you may include is to do something nice for a visitor or a caregiver. This may consist of asking them about their life, thanking them, or buying them a small gift. It is critical that you do not shut out other people at this time. Your love and communication with them is part of your spiritual growth and will assist you in attaining a peaceful transition.

Naturally, the most important activities I recommend you engage in at this time relate to the techniques given in chapter 10. I highly suggest you make tapes of those scripts and play them daily. The most important techniques for you are the before-death meditation, after-death meditation and conscious out-of-body experience. The others can be done less frequently.

The knowledge you obtain about your pending transition will help allay the usual anxieties. Remember, the number-one fear most people have is the fear of their own death. In my experience patients don't fear their transition, but they most certainly become anxious concerning their death. This is not merely a semantic difference in terms. It is a conscious change that may very well result in a conscious dying instead of an unconscious dying experience.

Returning to your daily schedule, this is the time in your life when you want to nourish the intimacies you cherish. Reading, thinking, pursuing creative hobbies, singing, looking at photographs, or calling long-lost friends are examples of some of the things you may decide to do at this time.

Do not compromise your basic rights just because you will shortly leave this world. You have the right to privacy. You have the right to demand information about your illness and what treatments are possible, and assurance that whatever is necessary for your comfort will be done. You have the right to undisturbed sleep and to comfort. You have a right to control as much as possible the day-to-day matters of your existence: foods, medicines, visitors, and how to spend your time. You are entitled to feel and express feelings, no matter how unpleasant they are to others. You have a right to develop spiritually in whatever direction you choose. These are only some of what I call your "Karmic Rights of Transition."

It is your responsibility to assert yourself and to inform your family that you want to be a part of the household in whatever degree you choose. Do not shut yourself out of the activities of your loved ones. Have them include you in their plans, even if it may occasionally be difficult or inconvenient for you. This may include having them share vacation plans that you won't be around to be a part of due to your transition.

There are many practical matters for you to consider at this time. You will have to decide on funeral arrangements, organ donation, wills or trusts, and other items specific to your situation. You will also have to decide on the disposition of personal possessions.

Because property squabbles can bring out the worst in families, taking charge of your legacy yourself is advisable. You may choose to give away jewelry, furniture, and other items to certain relatives and friends as tokens of your love and appreciation. Passing along various heirlooms establishes a sense of value and cohesiveness within a family. The easiest way to handle distribution of possessions is for you to make a list of all the things you value and to whom you would like to give them. If money or property is involved, I suggest you consult a lawyer or legal advice agency and make a will so that the disposition of your property will be clear and uncomplicated for heirs.

You should also be informed about any likely medical complications concerning your condition. A heart-to-heart talk with your family physician should be done at this time. Sometimes you need to appoint someone who can speak and act for you if you are unable to do so or are concerned that you soon may not be competent to represent yourself appropriately. The books noted in Appendix A will discuss these issues in greater detail.

Even with all the good intentions you have for dealing with your pending transition, the fact that a change in consciousness is on the horizon may bring on undue anxiety. The fallacies of what actually occurs to the body during its physical death are mostly responsible for this reaction. I would like to discuss this very sensitive topic of death from a medical viewpoint.

You will slowly fade away as physical death approaches. A feeling of weariness may be experienced if you are alert for several hours prior to this transition. Family members sense you as very far away. Most people actually die in their sleep and drift into their transition completely unaware of what is happening. It is quite rare for a dying patient to experience a suffocating or choking feeling prior to their death.

Certain physiological signs will be evident at the moment of death. The patient may make prolonged exhalations or take several short breaths and stop breathing entirely. The heart will cease beating. There is often a loss of bladder and bowel control. The patient will not respond to shouting or shaking the body, and their eyes will remain open and fixed on a certain spot. The mouth will open sightly and there may be a projection of air or waste from the body's orifices. The patient is now clinically dead.

Please keep in mind that your spirit or soul is very much alive at this time. Your soul has separated from its worn-out body, but your loved ones will always treasure your memory, and this will be facilitated by the presence of your soul. I encourage you to let go of ideas, things, places, people, and problems at this time. The conscious dying process will be facilitated by your understanding and application of this important principle. This will be easily accomplished by the conscious out-of-body experience technique.

UNFINISHED BUSINESS

Most people assume that death is permanent and irreversible. They recognize this universality and inevitability of death, but define it as a cessation of physiological functioning only. Dying and death are almost always viewed as something to be feared and avoided for as long as possible in our civilized culture.

Dying, especially conscious dying, is a tremendous opportunity for spiritual growth. I have worked with hundreds of dying patients, training them to make this transition consciously. What I have observed amounted to an empowerment reflected in these patients' ability to let go of their fears of death and face this voyage with a sense of pride, honor, and peace.

This is a time for completing unfinished business. By finishing business I am specifically referring to the ability to open up your heart and remove all resentments and fears. It is a form of forgiveness represented by the sending of love. To finish our business we must stop holding back. By removing the tendency to separate ourselves from others, but rather merge into a spiritual oneness, we can complete our business.

This principle is perfectly illustrated by our soul merging with our Higher Self at the moment of death. Conscious dying does just that. Finishing business is thus not to be looked upon as a balancing of some account by trying to rectify every mistake we may have made through our sojourns. The karmic principle of forgiveness makes this quite unnecessary.

The more we train our mind to function with clarity and compassion, the less we are hung up with the "I"-isms. The less superficial we are and the more we can experience our consciousness itself (Higher Self), the less we will cling to the very insecurities that lower the quality of our lives and keep us in this cycle of birth and death. It is not necessary to define who or what being is, just be one with it.

There is a metaphysical joke that I often tell at a workshop, "What is the only holistic vitamin on Earth? The answer is Vitamin B-1. If you can be one with your problem, then you are healed."

We cannot become whole if we are in pretense. Most relationships are shallow because we deny much of ourselves in dealing with others. We do this because we live our own lives as a facade. People are more concerned with doing the "right thing" and being "politically correct" than they are with personal empowerment.

How many of us do or say things that we really don't mean? How many of us act in a hypocritical fashion, only to use drugs or sex or some other distraction to repress the inevitable guilt from these actions? The term "love" is so overused that it has lost its real meaning. How many times has a parent or lover done something negative in the cause of "love"?

Most people have no more understanding of love than they do of jealousy, fear, joy, or anger. The "love" most commonly expressed is, in reality, a collection of needs and desires, moments of intense feelings and ecstasies incorrectly labeled.

The business of love is reflected more by feelings of guilt, possessiveness, jealousy, separateness, manipulations, neediness and other forms of insecurities. Self-protection is far more the business of love. It is always unfinished because until we recognize that love is a state of being and not merely an emotion, this love will always be conditional.

For love to be unconditional there must not be an "I" and "other." Unconditional love is not dualistic—it is oneness, a merging with our Higher Self. Only when we surrender our separateness into the universe and merge with our perfect energy can we love unconditionally. This is one of the goals of conscious dying. There is no unfinished business.

Many of my bereaved patients have unfinished business with a departed loved one. They feel it is too late to express their love to them now and feel guilty that they were not able to do so when they were alive. By training them to send love to the departed soul, this business can be completed. A superconscious mind tap, a future life progression, or an experience of conscious dying are but three techniques that can help facilitate this goal.

Jesus said, "Faith can move mountains." I say that love represents our wholeness of being which gives us the opportunity to eliminate our separateness and merge with the energy of our Higher Self and become one with the universe.

It is all too easy to get caught up in our lives and not see the forest for the trees. We forget that we are a part of the process. The new physics demonstrates that our consciousness creates this process and its various ramifications.

One solution is forgiveness. Forgiveness allows us to let go of this separateness, mostly represented as resentment. By feeling the pain of another and letting go of it through your heart, you can attain this result. The Maharaji said, "Don't put anyone out of your heart." You remove yourself when you do treat another this way. Jesus said it best, "Judge not, lest ye be judged."

It is our pride and resentment (manifestations of our ego) that block forgiveness. This results in our being closed to new experiences of growth. But being open to our perfect energy (Higher Self) and thus the true being of ourselves and others is the only true mechanism that will result in a real solution to this age-old problem of separateness and duality.

Forgiveness leads to compassion, and with compassion the pain evolves into love. The result is a merging into oneness. When we are one, there is no unfinished business.

The last point I want to discuss is a form of completion of your life. There are certain people in your life that you will want to say good-bye to and express your thanks for what they meant to you. Many of these people contributed to your accepting your prognosis and taking control of your life. This "transition empowerment" enabled you to enjoy more fully the last days of your life.

Some of these quality souls will stay by your side until the end, and these are usually the most difficult for you to say good-bye to. First, consider yourself fortunate to have these souls around you. Second, let them know how you feel, as this will shorten their bereavement period. Rejoice in the knowledge that you may eventually reunite with them, in another time and perhaps another dimension. This will facilitate both your and their eventual peaceful transition.

There is no experience
comparable…
than to be with someone
in their final hours

CHAPTER 17

Your Role as a Caregiver

Recent surveys show that four out of five people desire to die in their own home. In practice, eighty percent of people make this transition in an institution. It is highly preferable to die in one's home, in the midst of loved ones, pets, friends, and comfortable surroundings.

When one is at home, there is less fear of death. This often results in less need for pain medication. The resentments, jealousies, and petty quarrels that may have characterized family dynamics often disappear when a loved one is about to die.

The home setting can shorten the bereavement period of the surviving family and lessen their guilt feelings. There is no other experience comparable in its level of intimacy than to be with someone during their final hours. This almost always brings people together as no other circumstance can.

What is required at this time as a caregiver? The primary caregiver may already be living with the patient as child, parent, spouse, or friend; someone may volunteer or be recruited from among family, friends, or neighbors; or a housekeeper or health care worker may be hired through an agency, hospice, or personal recommendation. He or she must, above all, be someone the dying person likes and trusts. No special training or professional skills are needed, only the ability to be reliable, caring, and attentive to the patient's comfort. Everyone has the potential to care for another person and to do it well. Despite initial fears, caregivers come to realize that most of what is required are everyday skills. Whatever specialized abilities are necessary can be acquired with a little practice. Giving injections, monitoring a catheter, feeding an immobile patient, and giving a bed bath are easily learned.

Potential caregiver candidates often feel doubt as to whether they can accept and handle the responsibilities of this position. You can determine your ability to fulfill this role by answering affirmatively the following questions:

- Are you healthy and energetic?

- Are you flexible and able to adapt yourself to immediate needs?

- Are you organized and able to set priorities?

- Can you apply a sense of humor to awkward or embarrassing situations? Can you ease others' attitudes toward problems and stay with them when the going is rough?

- Do you enjoy being with people? Do you feel natural about offering help?

- Are you able to make the necessary time commitment or to solicit others to cover for you now and later when twenty-four-hour coverage is necessary?

- Are you able to welcome new ideas and suggestions from others? Do you enjoy learning new skills, asking questions, and learning how things work?

- Do you enjoy thinking of creative ways to solve problems? Do you take pleasure in applying "common sense" to a new challenge?

Potential caregivers may express doubts: They may fear that the relationship with the dying person will not stand up to the expected strain, or fear of the inability to hold up under the daily pressure of living with and caring for a dying person, including fear of being present at the time of death. Some will be fearful of things "medical" and the inability to provide sufficient medical care for the patient.

To fully understand these fears let us now examine them further. *Is your relationship with the dying patient strong enough?* Think about these questions.

- What do you like about each other?

- What is unique about your relationship?

- Have you shared crises before? How? What was good about your relationship during these occasions? What caused pressure?

- . What connects you?

- Do you feel secure about your bond?

You will learn more about what connects you as the days go by. No bond is without its complications. It may take only a chance comment to trigger an old unresolved anger between you and the patient. Remember that incidents like these are temporary and do not diminish the strength of your relationship. Our ability to understand and express ourselves at such times reinforces our connections to ourselves, the patient, and others.

Most caregivers say they had some anxieties about providing home care but they did it anyway and it was the right choice. Their fears and doubts were replaced with facts and experience.

Can I take the daily pressure? You will be told that giving injections, emptying bedpans, changing dressings, and other procedures are simple, but you may think they are not for you. Remember that while disease is undesirable, unpleasant, even dirty, the person suffering from it is not. Try to focus on your relationship and what you share with the patient, and see if this perspective overcomes the obstacles.

You can create a team of companions, professionals, and helpers who will run errands, visit, and advise you. You will find you've developed a new relationship with yourself. Providing home care is a rite of passage experience; each moment is full of new understanding and self-awareness, with opportunities to learn to care for yourself.

I'm not medically trained. There will probably not be anything very difficult about the medical care that is necessary. Most people and most homes are able to support terminal care. People who are dying usually do not require complicated equipment, and much of the nursing that will be necessary is similar to what you may have previously provided for yourself, your children, or sick friends.

You may experience fear of doing something that will harm or even kill the patient, a fear similar to that experienced by new mothers in caring for infants. To ease this anxiety, discuss your specific worries with the visiting nurse or doctor. Learn the patient's physical weaknesses and what dangers to expect.

Before you attempt home care for the patient you need to secure a physician who either personally or with associates will make home visits, provide twenty-four-hour consultations, and come to the house when the patient enters their transition. Many people experience difficulty in finding a doctor who will make house calls, especially on a weekend or in the middle of the night. It is important to get a commitment in advance.

If your own physician cannot or will not provide home care, ask for a referral. Your hospital, visiting nurse association, and medical association are all resources for the names of doctors who make home visits.

SPECIAL CONSIDERATIONS FOR THE DYING

- Keep a cassette player near the bed for the patient to listen to music, meditation tapes, or their self-hypnosis cassettes.

- Place a rope with a bell attached, or some other suitable signaling device, beside the bed so the patient can request help instantly.

- Keep water and juice available. Make sure they are frequently replaced with fresh supplies.

- Daily baths will assist in preventing bedsores.

- If bedpans are required, plastic is preferable to a metal one. Keeping metal bedpans warm is an added comfort.

- Turn the patient frequently to prevent them from developing bedsores. These sores most commonly appear on the buttocks, heels, and base of the spine.

- To prevent bowel discomforts, herbal laxative teas are highly useful. Enemas can be given as a last resort for constipation.

- A hot plate in the room will allow the patient to keep a cup of tea or coffee or a snack warm.

- For patients having difficulty in swallowing foods, liquid foods can be fed with a syringe or frozen into a popsicle.

- Hang dark curtains on the windows in the room so the patient can sleep during the day.

- A convenient, closely located bathroom is ideal for patients who are able to walk by themselves.

- Keep the room temperature constant at a level that is comfortable for them. There should be no drafts.

- Make sure there are non-slip rugs on the floor if the patient is using a walker.

- Have heating pads, hot water bottles, etc. readily available.

- A portable oxygen tank is helpful for patients having difficulty with their breathing. The physician will order this if it is needed.

- Placing side rails along the bed helps prevent the patient from accidentally falling from their bed when asleep.

- Consider having the patient stay in a living room or den rather than their bedroom. This allows the patients more access to social contacts. It may also give them the opportunity for more stimulating scenery. For a dying child, placing their bed in the living room can reduce their anxiety level. This way they need not fear that they are being sent to their room as a form of punishment.

- Keep a portable phone near the bed and within easy reach of the patient.

- Pen and writing pads should also be readily available in case the patient wants to jot down some thoughts or instructions for their caregivers.

- A cold washcloth on the patient's forehead and a gentle touch, such as holding their hand, helps reduce their anxiety.

- Keep several plants in the room. Also make sure family pets are available.

- Always be sensitive to the constantly changing condition of the patient. Be patient and tolerant of their wishes.

- Consider using a blender for such foods as "smoothies," ice cream, etc. This is especially indicated for patients who do not or cannot take in much bulky food at one time.

- Any supportive measure that can alleviate the patient's anxiety or feelings of guilt (they may feel their pending death is a punishment) is desirable.

In summary, place yourself in the patient's position. If it were you who was dying, what would you do to make this situation more comfortable? Be creative and sensitive in your preparations.

The ideal way to prepare for death is to practice conscious dying techniques throughout your life. For those loved ones of yours that do not have this training, there are still several things that you as a caregiver can do to facilitate this peaceful transition.

You can talk to the patient about the true nature of death and of consciousness. Give them a copy of this book or read selected passages to them. Eliminate the tendency to identify with the body. Be introspective. Look within your soul for answers. Do not be swayed by the projections of the five physical senses.

Practice the techniques given in chapter 10 with the patient, and continue with these techniques after their transition as instructed.

Be a giver, not a collector. Live the simple but quality life.

Be God-oriented, not world-oriented. Work at deeds to help others without expectation of some materialistic return as your main goal. Reduce your attachment to material objects. Be ready to lose them in time, if necessary. Nobody can take your soul.

Be informed about: the nature and mechanisms of consciousness; the true nature of death and of humanity; the laws of karma; the difference between conscious dying and unconscious dying; and the illusions of the physical world.

Practice spirituality at all times, under all kinds of circumstances, with every thought, feeling, word, and act. The following is a wonderful way to practice spirituality:

The Universal Code of Love

Practice harmlessness

Practice kindness

Practice friendship

Practice compassion

Practice serenity, peace

Practice care for all

Practice giving

Practice forgiving

Practice universal love

Practice reverence and respect

Practice altruism (non-egoism)

Practice humility

Practice praising, seeing the good in everything

Practice non-condemnation

Practice poverty of spirit, emptiness of heart

Practice purification

Practice loving the enemy, by blessing him, praying
    for him, and doing good to him

Practice self-sacrifice

Practice self-surrender

Practice selflessness

CHAPTER 17

WHEN DEATH FINALLY OCCURS

If a nurse or doctor is not present in the house at the time of death, call one immediately afterward. The nurse can confirm death, but a doctor is legally required to certify it. Call a friend or family member right away if you are alone. Don't wait to compose yourself or clean up; you need company. If you feel uncomfortable, stay on the telephone until someone arrives. When the person first dies and the body is still in the house, most people experience a huge silence, stillness, or absence.

Call the physician within an hour after the person dies. If the medical examiner or coroner must be notified, ask the physician to make this call for you. If there is to be an autopsy, or if the body or organs are being donated, call the hospital or medical school, tell them the patient has died, and arrange for transportation. You can wait to call the mortician or to remove the patient from the home. If you have made funeral arrangements in advance, notify the home when you want the body to be transported; if you have not, call a funeral home to begin making arrangements, or ask a member of the clergy or a friend to do so for you. Begin to call family and friends to let them know the person has died. If you don't know the plans for the funeral, try to provide them with a number to call, such as that of the funeral home or of a family friend, since you may not have the energy to make all those additional calls yourself.

Do not overlook the many people who have helped with care—who may not be close relatives or even related by blood, but who over the last days and weeks have become very close to the patient. Tired and grieving, they have been left by the one person who understood their commitment. Resentments that grow from being ignored by the family will isolate these individuals from the attention and emotional connections they deserve and feel. Include them in planning for the memorial or burial events. Encourage them to support each other and to stay in touch.

Part III

Conscious Dying—
A New Approach

...between-life consciousness
is as vital to our
immortal evolution as sleep is
to our physical well-being

CHAPTER 18

Historical Approaches to Conscious Dying

In this chapter you will find an overview of the history of conscious dying. This is not a product of the New Age; conscious dying has been around since the beginning of civilization.

The terms I use to describe my work with patients in preparing them for their peaceful transition may seem foreign to you. Terms such as "cleansing," "superconscious mind taps," "conscious out-of-body experience," "conscious dying," and "unconscious dying" may be unique to my practice, but the concept of conscious dying is at least 6,000 years old.

This chapter briefly traces the use of and reference to conscious dying from the ancient Egyptians to modern times, then presents a detailed account of some of the more significant examples of ancient texts and metaphysical theory concerning this most unusual discipline.

The very concept of conscious dying seems to most Westerns so foreign an idea that they find it incredible that the concept has been presented to them in many different ways throughout their lives. I have previously mentioned the Masses of the Catholic Church, especially Requiem Masses (more on these in chapter 22).

Hollywood has indirectly contributed to a disguised form of this concept in their mummy movies. The term "Mystery Schools" was not mentioned but the principles on conscious dying were most certainly illustrated. When the celluloid high priest prepared the Tana leaves for the mummy (often Boris Karloff), he was conducting an initiation characteristic of the Egyptian Mystery Schools (see chapter 21). I am the first to acknowledge the fact that there was considerable creative license used in these depictions.

Westerners do not relate well to the term Mystery Schools. We may briefly have read about this ritual in our history courses, but unless a special interest and much outside reading is undertaken, this concept falls on deaf ears.

I must admit to my lack of knowledge concerning *The Egyptian Book of the Dead*[1] until I became involved in metaphysics. *The Tibetan Book of the Dead*[2] also results in blank stares from most of the people to whom I mention that book, but there are some who have heard of it. I deal with the Tibetan text first, in chapter 19, because of its relative familiarity. Chronologically, *The Egyptian Book of the Dead* comes first but apparently not in the heart and soul of Westerners..

HISTORIC OVERVIEW OF CONSCIOUS DYING

The *Egyptian Book of the Dead* (chapter 20) is the first known guidebook for the afterlife. Dating back to 1300 B.C., its original Egyptian title was *Going Forth in Light*. The predominant feature characteristic of entry into the between-life state was a blinding light.

The Egyptians prepared their dead to enter the next dimension by burying such useful items as weapons, clothing, and cooking utensils to satisfy any earthly cravings the earthbound discarnate entity might have.

---

1   Budge, 1895.
2   Evans-Wentz, 1960.

There are three chambers inside the Great Pyramid in Egypt. Many feel that these chambers represent the conscious mind, the subconscious mind, and the superconscious mind. The royal sarcophagus lay in the King's Chamber, the uppermost room (superconscious mind). Many people have lain inside this sarcophagus and have described their experience as a transcendent one. This form of conscious dying was reportedly used by the ancient Egyptians.

Servants of a Sumerian household, a society that flourished 3,400 years before Christ north of the Persian Gulf, were slain when their master died so that they might retain their role in the next incarnation.

The belief in reincarnation and conscious dying is an extension and adjustment to Darwinian evolution. The ancient Druids of 2,500 years ago taught that conscious dying is the path to enlightenment, and that a soul will not attain this goal until it learns these techniques and principles.

The Ancient Mystery Schools of Egypt, Persia, China, Greece, and other lands (see chapter 21) dealt with conscious dying techniques. Europe retained these teachings throughout the Middle Ages and the Renaissance. Various primitive churches of Christendom, notably the Roman, Greek, Anglican, Syrian, Armenian, and Coptic, and other churches dating from Reformation days wisely incorporated into their rituals and observances many principles of this pre-Christian Art of Dying (see chapter 22).

These churches continue to maintain these efforts today, in contrast to modern medicine. Medicine offers no guidance for the dying, but mechanically sustains life at any cost to the soul. Narcotic drugs given to patients, along with the fears of co-dependency projected, offer no spiritual growth for the soul at its most defining moment, that of death.

The soul was thought to wander in between lives, a theme persistent in religious traditions ranging from Chinese Buddhism to esoteric Christianity. The Greek philosopher Plato stated: "Every soul...is ordained to wander between incarnations in the region between the moon and the Earth...."[3]

---

3   Plato. *Euthyphro* in *A Guided Tour of Five Works of Plato* (Mountain View, CA: Mayfield Pub., 1988).

The *Katha Upanishad* in India, which dates back to the sixth century B.C., averred: "The Self…does not die when the body dies. Concealed in the heart of all beings lies the atma, the Spirit, the Self; smaller than the smallest atom, greater than the great spaces."[4]

Other common features of this between-life state found in mythological and scriptural writings are the presence of a bright light, a sense of timelessness, and a panoramic review of the past life and the soul's judgment, often accompanied by three wise figures.

Does this not remind you of the core experience Dr. Raymond Moody first described in his classic book, *Life After Life?*[5] We have already discussed this core experience in chapter 2.

The ancients, including Pythagoras, Plato, Plotinus, Krishna, Buddha, the Gnostic Christians, the Druids of the Celtic world, and the Hierophants of the Ancient Mystery Schools of Egypt, Greece, Rome, Persia, and China, all held to the doctrine of reincarnation and conscious dying.

In the Palazzo Ducale in Venice, Italy, are four portraits by the Dutch painter Hieronymus Bosch (1450–1516), known collectively as *Visions of the Hereafter*. Figure 4 (page 155) is one of the panels titled "Ascent into the Empyrium." The Empyrium was considered the highest heaven in medieval cosmology. This is a 500-year-old depiction of the core experience of an NDE.

OTHER GUIDEBOOKS FOR CONSCIOUS DYING

Conscious dying techniques have been recorded in The *De Arte Morendi* and other similar medieval treatises on the craft of dying, the Orphic Manual called *The Descent into Hades* and other guide-books for the use of the dead, the *Pretakhanda* of the Hindu *Garuda Purana*, Swedenborg's *De Coelo et de Inferno*, Rusca's *De Inferno*, and several other eschatological works, both ancient and modern. The *Garuda Purana* of India

---

4   Swami Premananda. *Katha Upanishad: Dialogue of Death and Vision of Immortality* (Washington, DC: Self Realization Fellowship, 1943).

5   Moody, 1981.

Figure 4
Ascent into the Empyrium, detail from *Visions of the Hereafter*
Painting by Hieronymus Bosch, Palazzo Ducale, Venice, Italy. Printed with permission:
Alinari/Art Resource, New York.

deals with the rites used over the dying, the death-moment, the funeral ceremonies, the building up, by means of the *Pretashraddha* rite, of a new body for the *Preta* or deceased in lieu of that destroyed by fire, the Judgment and the various states through which the deceased passes until he is reborn again on earth.

THE TIBETAN BOOK OF THE DEAD

According to W. Y. Evans-Wentz, "Buddhists and Hindus alike believe that the last thought at the moment of death determines the character of the next incarnation."[6] Writings like the *Bardo Thödol*, or *The Tibetan Book of the Dead*, as it is better known in the West, are intended to direct the thought processes of the dying person during the transitional period of life-death-rebirth. This text has served as a guide for the living as well as the dying since the eighth century A.D.

The term "bardo" is used to describe the gap or interval between birth and death. The *Bardo Thödol* instructs one on how to use these experiences to awaken to a more enlightened incarnation. Some of these bardo occurrences are pleasant, while others are horrifying. The experiencer (recently departed soul) wakes up out of one "swoon" or trance state and enters into a succeeding bardo until he/she finally reincarnates.

The horrifying experiences are clearly labeled as illusions created by the experiencer's own projections. The desirability is emphasized throughout this ancient text to maintain consciousness at the moment of death to ease the transition into a new life. The bardo is described as follows: ". . . you have no physical body of flesh and blood, so whatever sounds, colors, and rays of light occur, they cannot hurt you and you cannot die…Know this to be the bardo state."

A detailed description of this book will be given in chapter 19.

---

6 Evans-Wentz, 1960.

EAST MEETS WEST

The origin of the Roman Catholic concept of purgatory is often credited to the ancient Greek description of a discarnate soul between incarnations. According to Rudolf Steiner, the founder of anthroposophy, the purgatory of the Catholic Church is a recognizable, if seriously inaccurate, picture of the initial stages of the between-life state where the soul weans itself of all desires, appetites, and passions. Steiner, whose knowledge of disembodied existence was gained through clairvoyance, had much to say about the plane of consciousness between lives, insisting that "life between death and rebirth is...a continuation of the life here." To Steiner, death was simply a means of restoration and rejuvenation. "In order to sustain consciousness and to keep it active," he wrote, "we have been continually destroying our corporeal sheath." He was making the point that between-life consciousness is as vital to our immortal evolution as sleep is to our physical well-being.

Another interesting meeting of the Eastern and Western mind regarding dying is that both the Catholic and Hindu last rites involve constant prayer and repetition of sacred names. However, there is a great deal of difference between the Western approach to death and immortality versus its Eastern counterpart.

Dualism appears to predominate in Western thought. An experience is analyzed as being either this or that. Differences are established and contrasts are made. Thus, life is opposed to death. Whereas life represents "good," death is the enemy of life and must therefore be "evil."

Easterners emphasize the integrity of the whole rather than the differences between component parts. To them unity underlies what may appear to be contradictory phenomena. They promote the concept that such apparent contrasts are merely illusory aspects of an undivided reality.

...when a soul dies
in the meditative samadhi state
...liberation from the
karmic cycle is assured

CHAPTER 19

The Tibetan Book of the Dead

T he *Tibetan Book of the Dead*,[1] also known as the *Bardo Thödol*, is a
    guide written for and by Tibetan monks and devout lay people to
incorporate a lifetime of practice into the moment of transition we call
death. It is meant to make the unfamiliar familiar and to reinforce visualization techniques that may have been practiced for years. It is perhaps the best-known example of the literature that exists in almost
every culture on the journey through after-death states.

By emphasizing the fact that the mind creates many illusions about
death, this text attempts to alleviate separatist feelings that bring about
fear. Its goal is to let go of the false and train the transitee to merge with
their Higher Self.

The term "bardo" refers to the intermediate experiences of
between-life and rebirth. There are six bardos described. These books
represent only seven of the seventeen chapters of the entire work. They
are accounts of the Mahayana Buddhist tradition, specifically its northern mystical tantric path to "instantaneous enlightenment." These

---

1   Evans-Wentz, 1960.

books describe the dying, between-life, and rebirth processes, as revealed through enlightened lamas.

The text, written during the eighth and eleventh centuries A.D., is comprised of three parts. The first part, called '*Chi-kha'i Bardo*, describes the psychic happening at the moment of death. The second part, or *Chos-nyid Bardo*, deals with the dream-state which supervenes immediately after death, and with what are called "karmic illusions." The third part, or *Srid-pa'i Bardo*, concerns the onset of the birth-instinct and of prenatal events. The purpose of the instruction is to fix the attention of the deceased, at each successive stage of delusion and entanglement, on the ever-present possibility of liberation, and to explain to him or her the nature of their visions. The text of the *Bardo Thödol* is recited by the lama in the presence of the corpse.

The first bardo is the Bardo of Birth. The Lifetime Bardo is the next one described. This bardo deals with the entire lifetime on the physical plane. The third bardo is the bardo of the Moments Before Death.

The Bardo of the Moments After Death constitutes the fourth bardo. From these last two bardos you can see how the concept of death has no basis in reality to the Tibetans. There is no death bardo, merely those just moments before and after what we term as death. The body is not assumed to be alive on its own, but rather dependent on the "life force." This life force is withdrawn when the physical body dies and the reverse applies during birth. It is during this fourth bardo that the soul encounters the great light called the Dharmata.

The fifth bardo is the Deathtime Bardo. This is a time of wandering and of learning. Many peaceful and wrathful deities are encountered by the soul at this time. The Bardo of the Moment Before Birth is the sixth and final bardo. It deals with choosing a new body and reincarnating.

These books were initially prepared for people who had proficiently practiced meditation throughout their life. It was intended to guide them to see that everything in life and death is illusory and dualistic, in order that they might become an enlightened Buddha. In the instance of someone less adept, its purpose was to guide the voyager through death and rebirth with an unbroken stream of consciousness (connection to their Higher Self), allowing them to consciously remember their past lives and learn lessons in their next life. This liberating process is called the "transference." It was achieved through a practice called *Phowa*, in which the life force is moved out through the top of the head, used in conjunction with the reading of a book of the dead.

It is thought that when a person dies while in the meditative samadhi state they practiced throughout their life, their soul's liberation from the karmic cycle is assured. The thoughts at the point of death are crucial in determining the quality of the bardo experience.

In the West, the term bardo is erroneously used to refer only to the period between lives—the "intermediate state." The Eastern definition implies that it alludes to any of six transitional and illusory states of consciousness: waking, dreaming, profound meditation, dying, experiencing reality between lives, and rebirth. Enlightenment, or liberation, is possible at any juncture in any of these bardos through similar means, including practices described in the books of the dead, because all of the bardos share the same quality of being transitional.

The 'Chi-kha'i and Chos-nyid Bardos are essentially a sequence of "tests" of a person's understanding of and meditative experience in the nature of reality and the nature of one's true self, beyond the ego-self. Opportunities for growth in awareness of reality and the self are provided by these challenges.

In the 'Chi-kha'i and Chos-nyid Bardos, the soul experiences a series of tests which represent its karma. Each aspect of the mind is perceived as a light or as a Buddha emitting a light from his heart. By responding favorably to this light during the first eight days of bardo, the soul has a good chance of attaining liberation. If the soul responds with fear or is attracted to a lower level of consciousness, the soul would then experience lower and darker levels of consciousness. The soul would seek a comfortable level and be reborn at that lower level with much karma to overcome.

A person may remain more or less conscious through the above dying process, depending on how practiced he or she is in yogic meditation. Skillful meditators are said to experience a "swoon"—a temporary loss of consciousness—during the second half of the dawning of the mind of near-black attainment. Their consciousness is regained with the dawning of the clear light.

The Tibetan Book of the Dead teaches that each of the transitions between the bardos of waking, experiencing reality, and rebirth, as well as before and after the bardo of sleeping and dreaming, are constituted by forward dissolution and then reaggregation into a physical, subtle, or dream body. Thus, each bardo is separated from others by a swoon. This belief agrees with the occurrence of the dark void in NDEs, and the interpretation of the void as the mind's representation of a transition between states of consciousness.

In the ideal case, the guru or lama who has been tracking the departed soul's progress reads from *The Tibetan Book of the Dead*. The voyager is reminded of their training and encouraged to merge with the clear light, as this light is their true self—this merging will create Dharma-kaya, and the soul will be liberated.

Unfortunately, most voyagers fail to do this. The result is a fading of the clear light of pure consciousness. The tests now continue.

The transitee will meet various peaceful and wrathful Buddhas as part of their tests. The wrathful Buddha is the dark side of one of the peaceful Buddhas. The wrathful Buddhas appear in the same order as their peaceful counterparts. The person is instructed to recognize these, too, as aspects of their consciousness, and to unite with them. In merging with a wrathful Buddha, the person will obtain Buddhahood and spend their remaining between-life time in the peaceful, divine realm of mind associated with the peaceful counterpart of the wrathful Buddha. In running away, the person will only fall into deeper and more terrifying levels of the intermediate state.

On the thirteenth and fourteenth days, the person who has not recognized the darker sides of themselves represented by the wrathful Buddhas perceives fifty-eight other wrathful deities (including eight Gaurima, eight Takenma, four doorkeepers, and twenty-eight Wang Chuk Ma). If these are not recognized, then all of the wrathful deities appear jointly as the Lord of Death. The Lord of Death dismembers the person, who, despite great pain, cannot die. This symbolizes the difficulty of extinguishing the lesser ego-self as the person clings to this self-image. The hellish torments of the Chos-nyid state are described in the text as follows:

> Then the Lord of Death will place round thy neck a rope and drag thee along; he will cut off thy head, tear out thy heart, pull out thy intestines, lick up thy brain, drink thy blood, eat thy flesh, and gnaw thy bones; but thou wilt be incapable of dying. Even when thy body is hacked to pieces, it will revive again. The repeated hacking will cause intense pain and torture.[2]

In the *Srid-pa'i Bardo*, the person finds that they have a body similar in form to that in their previous life, but of extraordinary powers. All senses are heightened. The person is capable of traveling instantly wherever they wish, passing through solids, and appearing to change their form. Yet the person does not realize they are dead. The person sees his or her home and relatives in mourning and tries to contact them and convince them that he or she is still alive. When communication is impossible and the person feels like an outcast, the person comes to realize for the first time that he or she is dead.

Later the soul is judged by the Lord of Death and two "Geniuses" (guardian beings), who count out the person's good and bad deeds with white and black pebbles. Lying about one's deeds is not possible because the Lord of Death, who is symbolic of one's guilt, looks into the Mirror of Karma, where one's deeds are vividly reflected, symbolic of one's memory. The Lord of Death then again dismembers the person who, despite intense pain, cannot die. This situation represents the difficulty that one's ego has in dealing with the dark sides of oneself.

Next, the person sees their own funeral and division of inheritance. Interference in these matters will cause the person to be born in the plane of unhappy ghosts. In contrast, those who have accumulated good karma have delightful experiences throughout the Strid-pa'i Bardo. Finally, as rebirth approaches, colors associated with the six planes of sasnsara shine from them. The person is attracted to the color

---

2   Ibid.

of the plane in which they are to be reborn and experiences entering a corresponding landscape, such as a heavenly palace, a lovely garden, a place of natural beauty, or a cave. The person's subtle body fades and takes on the color of that plane of rebirth.

As the person passes through lower and lower levels of the Chos-nyid and Srid-pa'i Bardos, there is a change in the means by which release can be obtained from experiences in those levels into more pleasant levels or states of mind. Knowledge of the Self and meditation are effective in the first thirteen days of the Chos-nyid Bardo. Devotion, faith, and prayer are effective when facing the Lord of Death on the fourteenth day. Remembering compassion is effective in the Srid-pa'i Bardo.

In the final phases of the Srid-pa'i Bardo, the person enters a womb and is reborn. This entire process takes forty-nine days from the first bardo until the sixth is completed. *The Tibetan Book of the Dead* teaches the transitee to face death calmly, heroically, and with a clear mind.

ANALYSIS

The *Bardo Thödol* is far more important than merely a religious speculation about death and a hypothetical after-death state. It is a guide for those who are seeking a spiritual path of soul liberation. *The Tibetan Book of the Dead* was originally designed to aid the living as well.

This text simply does not appeal to Westerners who neither identify with the mechanism nor relate to the theological constructs. My own surveys show that those Americans who even recognize the name of this book unfortunately have not the slightest idea of its purpose.

Originally, the *Bardo Thödol* were hidden for later preservation, probably due to the persecution of Buddhists by Langdarma during the early ninth century A.D. Many of these buried scriptures were recovered during the succeeding centuries and designated Termas, a term derived from the Tibetan word *gter*, meaning "treasure." Those who discovered these spiritual treasures and propagated their teachings were called *Tertons*, from Tibetan *gter-bston*, meaning "revealer of treasure."

Some Western critics claim these Tertons were responsible for writing the scriptures. These skeptics accuse the *Bardo Thödol* of being forged by people who wanted to pass off their own ideas under the guise of ancient revelations. Nothing could be further from the truth.

It is a mortal sin for a Tibetan to add or delete so much as a single letter from the Sacred Scriptures. In addition, the forging would require a technical and critical knowledge of history and linguistics such as was not only unknown in Tibet, but that would have required a mastermind for its execution. Had a genius of that sort existed in Tibet, he would have had no need to resort to the subterfuge of forgery, for he could have stood on his own feet, as did many scholarly geniuses who wrote and taught in their own name. These scriptures consisted of 108 volumes. This fact makes the accusation even more absurd.

The dead or dying person is addressed in the *Bardo Thödol* for three reasons: (1) the initiate needs to be reminded of his or her spiritual preparation for death, especially if they lack alertness during this critical time; (2) the dying person needs to be surrounded with helpful thoughts during the initial stages of bardo without allowing emotional attachments to depress their spirit; and (3) the voyager should treat every moment of his or her life as if it were the last. Thus, one function of the *Bardo Thödol* is to assist the remaining loved ones so they in turn will not deviate from their own karmic path.

We have nothing in the West comparable to the *Bardo Thödol*, except for certain secret writings inaccessible to the wider public and to the ordinary scientist. The Catholic Church is the only structure where provision is made for the souls of the departed. Inside the Protestant camp, with its world-affirming optimism, are a few mediumistic "rescue circles" whose main concern is to make the dead aware that they *are* dead.

Apart from the masses said for the soul in the Catholic Church, the provisions we make for the dead are rudimentary and on the lowest level, not because we cannot convince ourselves of the soul's immortality, but because we have rationalized out of existence the psychological need of the living to do something for the departed. Because we cannot believe in a life after death we prefer to do nothing about it. Simpler-minded people follow their own feelings, and, as in Italy, build themselves funeral monuments of gruesome beauty. Catholic masses for the soul, because they are expressly intended for the psychic welfare of the deceased, are not a mere gratification of lachrymose sentiments.

Empowerment is the ultimate goal of the *Bardo Thödol*. Thereby the initiated disciple attains dominion over the realm of death, and, being able to perceive death's illusory nature, is freed from fear. This illusoriness of death comes from the identification of the individual with his temporal, transitory form, whether physical, emotional, or mental, from which arises the mistaken notion that there exists a personal, separate egohood of one's own, and the fear of losing it.

If, however, the voyager has identified him- or herself with the Absolute, the Dharma, then the fears of death disappear. He or she now realizes that all they are exposed to is but a reflection of their own conscious and subconscious mental content; and no mind-created illusion can then have power over them if they know its origin and are able to recognize it. This is what the *Bardo Thödol* teaches.

This text actually reveals the secret life under the guise of a science of death—by far its greatest value spiritually. One must applaud the efforts of Lama Kazi Dawa-Samdup and Dr. Evans-Wentz as the first translators of the *Bardo Thödol*. It was with a true form of dedication and commitment that they approached their work.

They realized that their work could not be considered final, but merely a starting point for even more perfect translations. This was unquestionably a sacred trust, handed down over 1,000 years, which needed to be treated with the utmost respect, even to the smallest detail. Westerners could relate this to the history of the Old and New Testaments and their preservation over the centuries.

The world truly owes a debt of gratitude to these two scholars. Lama Kazi Dawa-Samdup was the chief interpreter on the staff of His Excellency Lonchen Satra, the Tibetan Plenipotentiary to the government of India. He was also attached to the political staff of His Holiness, the Dalai Lama, on the latter's visit to India. At the time of his death Lama Kazi Dawa-Samdup was Lecturer in Tibetan to the University of Calcutta.

Those who have lain down
rise up to look upon thee,
they breathe the air
...their hearts are at peace

CHAPTER 20

The Egyptian Book of the Dead

The ancient title of *The Book of the Dead*[1] was *Chapters for Coming Forth by Day.* This text was the result of a long and tedious faith and ritual practice beginning around 1580 B.C. The *Pyramid Texts* and *Coffin Texts* preceded it and were undoubtedly used as sources for the *Book of the Dead.*

The purpose of this book was to help the departed rise to life again and attain fulfillment in the next world. It involved many strange and complex ideas about destiny and human nature.

Egyptian thought was first made known to us through the *Pyramid Texts,* hieroglyphic characters inscribed on the walls of certain pyramids in Sakkara, the burial place for the ancient city of Memphis. These texts date from 2350 to 2175 B.C., but contain material from earlier periods.

It was the priests at Heliopolis that arranged these inscriptions for the sun god, Amen-Ra (or Ra). The priests' purpose was to provide the kings buried in these pyramids with the magical means of securing

---

1 Budge, 1895.

resurrection from death and ascent to the sky, where they might join the sun god on his unending journey through the sky by day and the underworld by night. The sun god was imagined to make this journey by boat, and in the Egyptian mind eternal bliss was thus conceived as being forever in the company of Ra as he made his unceasing circuit of the universe.

Ra was assumed to be the creator of the universe and Heliopolis the place where the universe began. The *Pyramid Texts* include rituals for embalming and funeral rites, magical spells, myths, hymns, prayers and incantations. The priests associated the pharaoh's eternal fate with that of Ra. They also recognized the god Osiris, a good king of the past who had risen from the dead after being murdered. Thus, by identifying the pharaoh with Osiris, the returning to life again of the departed king was assured.

In *The Book of the Dead* (xvii–109 ff.) we find that the Soul of Ra and the Soul of Osiris together form the double divine soul which inhabited the TCHAFI, who dwelt in Tettu. The existence of a World-Soul presupposed the existence of a World-Body, which is the material universe; and the embodiment of this was, according to the priests of Heliopolis, the body of Osiris. Men and gods were supposed to contain the same component parts. Man possessed a physical body (*khat*); a soul (*ba*); a heart (*ab*); a double (*ka*); an intelligence (*khu*); power (*sekhem*); a shadow (*khaibit*); a spiritual body (*sah*); a name (*ren*); and the gods possessed divine counterparts of all these.

Osiris is a god and judge of the dead, as well as the symbol of resurrection. *The Book of the Dead* considers Osiris the greatest of the gods as the arbiter of future destiny. As a mortal being, he was murdered and dismembered. Later his limbs became reconstituted and his immortality was assured. Remarkably, Osiris' body never decayed.

Osiris' body was embalmed by Horus, Anubis, and Isis, who carried out with the greatest care and exactitude all the prescriptions which had been ordered by Thoth, and who performed their work so thoroughly that the material body which Osiris possessed on this earth served as the body for the god in the world beyond the grave, though only after it had undergone some mysterious change, brought about by the words of power which these gods said and by the ceremonies which they performed. A very ancient tradition declared that the god Thoth himself had acted the part of priest for Osiris, and although the Egyptians believed that it was his words that brought the dead god back to life, they were never able wholly to free themselves from the idea that the series of magical ceremonies that they performed in connection with the embalmment and burial of the dead produced most beneficial results for their deceased friends.

The compositions that form the chapters of *The Book of the Dead* are declared to have been written by Thoth, and they were assumed to be identical with those that this god pronounced on behalf of Osiris. The Egyptians believed that the resurrected Osiris could give life after death to anyone since he himself had attained this state. Osiris could give eternal life to the souls of men in their transformed bodies because he had made himself incorruptible and immortal. Moreover, he was himself "Eternity and Everlastingness," and it was he who "made men and women to be born again." The new birth was the birth into the new life of the world that is beyond the grave and is everlasting. Osiris could give life because he was life, he could make man to rise from the dead because he was the resurrection; but the priesthood taught in all periods of Egyptian history that it was necessary to endeavor to obtain the favor of the god by means of magical and religious words and ceremonies. From the earliest times the belief in the immortality of Osiris existed, and the existence of the dead after death was bound up with that of the god.

The famous "Judgment Scene" of *The Book of the Dead* is contained in the Papyrus of Ani, currently held by the British Museum. This plate depicts Osiris in his role as the judge of the dead. The ancient Egyptians believed that the souls of the dead were judged by Osiris. They represented this judgment pictorially as a pair of scales weighing the heart, from which they declared all thoughts and actions emanated. They were simply too logical to think that words or actions could be weighed by a material balance. The word "MAAT" was used to depict

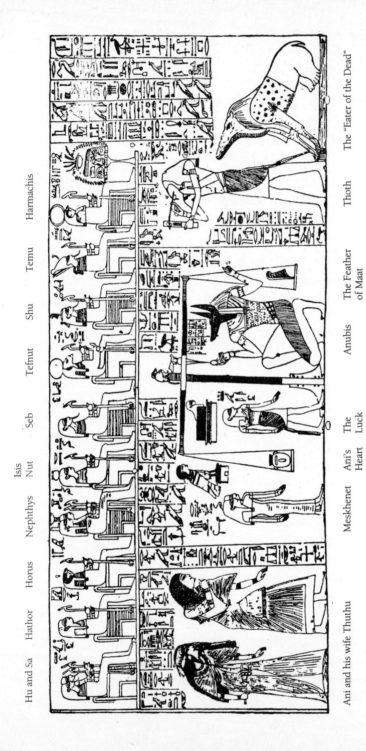

Hu and Sa   Hathor   Horus   Nephthys   Isis / Nut   Seb   Tefnut   Shu   Temu   Harmachis

Ani and his wife Thuthu   Meskhenet   Ani's Heart   The Luck   Anubis   The Feather of Maat   Thoth   The "Eater of the Dead"

Figure 5
The Judgment

(from *The Egyptian Book of the Dead*, E. A. Walllis Budge, Barnes & Noble, Inc.)

right, truth, law, and rectitude. It was against this emblem of MAAT (the feather) that they placed the heart. Either a heart or the entire body was weighed against this feather.

The judgment of each individual seems to have taken place soon after death, and annihilation or everlasting life and bliss to have been decreed at once for the souls of the dead. The ancient Egyptians did not believe in either a general resurrection or a prolonged punishment.

The Judgment Scene (see page 170) as given in the Papyrus of Ani may be thus described:

> The scribe Ani and his wife Thuthu enter the Hall of Maati, wherein the heart, symbolic of the conscience, is to be weighed in the balance against the feather, emblematic of right and truth. In the upper register are the gods who sit in judgment, and who form the great company of the gods of Heliopolis, to whom are added Hathor, Hu, and Sa. On the standard of the Balance sits the dog-headed ape, the companion of Thoth, the scribe of the gods; and the god Anubis, jackal-headed, examines the pointer to make certain that the beam is exactly horizontal, and that the tongue of the balance is in its proper place. On the left of the Balance are: SHAI, the god of luck, or destiny; The MESKHEN, or rectangular object with a human head that rests upon a pylon, and is commonly thought to be connected with the place of birth; MESKHENET, the goddess of the funeral chamber, and RENENET, the goddess of nursing. The soul of Ani is in the form of a human-headed hawk standing upon a pylon. The lines of hieroglyphics which appear above the figures of Ani and his wife contain a version of Chapter XXXB of *The Book of the Dead*, in which the deceased addresses his heart, and prays that the sovereign chiefs may not oppose his judgment, and that it may not be separated from him in the presence of the keeper of the Balance. The sovereign chiefs here referred to are Mestha, Hapi, Tuamutef, and Qebhsennuf, the children of Horus. After the heart has been weighed, Thoth, being satisfied with the result, addresses the gods, saying:

CHAPTER 20

"The heart of Osiris Ani hath indeed been weighed, and his soul hath borne witness concerning him (or it); it hath been found true by trial in the Great Balance. No evil hath been found in him, he hath not wasted the offerings in the temples, he hath not done harm by his deeds, and he hath uttered no evil report whilst he was upon earth."

In answer to these words the gods ratify the sentence of Thoth, and they declare that he is holy and righteous, and that he hath not sinned against them; therefore the monster AMEMET, or the "Eater of the dead," who is seen standing behind Thoth, shall not prevail over him, and they further decree that he shall have a homestead in Sekhet-hetepu forever, and that offerings shall be made to him, and that he shall have the power to appear before Osiris at will.

In his speech, the son of Isis (Horus) says: "I have come to thee, O Un-nefer, and I have brought unto thee the Osiris Ani. His heart is righteous, and it hath come forth innocent from the Balance; it hath not sinned against any god or any goddess. Thoth hath weighed it according to the decree pronounced unto him by the company of the gods; and it is most true and righteous. Grant that cakes and ale may be given unto him, and let him appear in the presence of Osiris; and let him be like unto the followers of Horus for ever and ever."

The scribe Ani then makes his prayer to Osiris in the following words: "Behold I am in thy presence, O lord of Amentet. There is no sin in my body. I have not spoken that which is not true knowingly, nor have I done aught with a false heart. Grant thou that I may be like unto those favoured ones who are in thy following, and that I say be an Osiris greatly favoured of the beautiful god, and beloved of the lord of the world, [I] who am indeed a royal scribe, who loveth thee, Ani MAA KHERU before the god Osiris."[2]

Osiris' reply is not recorded, but it is assumed that Ani's petition was granted and Ani was free to pass into all the various regions of the dominion of Osiris, and to enter into everlasting life and happiness.

---

2   Ibid.

In the description of the Judgment Scene given above, reference is made to the Eater of the Dead, and in connection with him it must be observed that he was supposed to devour straightway the souls of all those who were condemned in the Judgment Hall of Osiris, and that from one point of view the punishment of the wicked consisted of annihilation. Before a man who is MAA KHERU, every door of the Underworld opened itself, and every hostile power, animate or inanimate, was made to remove itself from his path.

In *The Book of the Dead* (the Rubric to Chapter CLXII) an address is made to the god Amen-Ra for the purpose of retaining heat in the body of the deceased. An amulet is placed under the head of the deceased and the following is stated: "O Amen, O Amen, who art in heaven, turn thy face upon the dead body of thy son, and make him sound and strong in the Underworld."[3]

The third passage of Chapter CLXV is a petition to Amen-Ra by the deceased wherein the most powerful of the magical names of the gods are enumerated. The vignette of the chapter contains the figure of an ithyphallic god with the body of a beetle; on his head are the characteristic plumes of Amen, and his right arm is raised like that of Amsu, or Min, the god of the reproductive powers of nature. It reads:

> Hail, thou BEKHENNU Bekhennu! Hail, Prince, Prince! Hail Amen, Hail Amen! Hail PAR, Hail IUKASA! Hail God, Prince of the gods of the eastern parts of heaven, AMEN-NATHEK-ERETHI-AMEN.... Hail, Amen, let me make supplication unto thee, for I know thy name, and [the mention of] thy transformations in my mouth, and thy skin is before mine eyes. Come, I pray thee, and place thou thine heir and thine image, myself, in the everlasting underworld. Grant thou that all my members may repose in Neter-khertet (the underworld), or (as others say) in Akertet (the underworld); let my whole body become like unto that of a god.[4]

3, 4 Ibid.

In the Saite Recension of *The Book of the Dead* the following address is given:

> Oh Amen, O Amen, O God, O God, O Amen, I adore thy name, grant thou to me that I may understand thee; grant thou that I may have peace in the Tuat (underworld), and that may possess all my members therein. And the divine Soul which is the Nut saith, "I will make my divine strength to protect thee, and I will perform everything which thou hast said." This interesting text was ordered to be recited over a figure of the "god of the lifted hand," i.e., of Amen in his character of the god of generation and reproduction, painted blue, and the knowledge of it was to be kept from the god SUKATI in the Tuat; if the directions given in the rubric were properly carried out it would enable the deceased to drink water in the underworld from the deepest and purest part of the celestial stream, and he would become "like the stars in the heavens above."[5]

From the Papyrus of Ani (sheet 2) we find the following hymn to Osiris:

> GLORY BE TO THEE, OSIRIS UN-NEFER, the great god who dwellest within Abtu (Abydos), thou king of eternity, thou lord of everlastingness, who passest through millions of years in the course of thine existence. Thou art the eldest son of the womb of Nut, and thou wast engendered by Seb, the Ancestor (erpat); thou art the lord of the crowns of the South and North, thou art the lord of the lofty white crown, and as prince of gods and men thou hast received the crook, and the whip, and the dignity of his divine fathers. Let thine heart, O Osiris, who art in the Mountain of Amentet, be content, for thy son Horus is established upon thy throne. Thou art crowned lord of Tettu (Mendes), and ruler in Abtu (Abydos). Through thee the world waxeth green in triumph before the might of Neb-er-tcher. He leadeth in his train that which is and that which is not yet, in his name Ta-her-sta-nef; he toweth along the earth by Maat in

---

5 Ibid.

his name of 'Seker'; he is exceedingly mighty and most terrible in his name 'Osiris'; he endureth for ever and for ever in his name of 'Un-nefer.

Homage be to thee, O King of kings, Lord of lords, Ruler of princes, who from the womb of Nut has ruled the world and the Underworld (Akert). Thy members are [like] bright and shining copper, thy head is blue [like] lapis-lazuli, and the greenness of the turquoise is on both sides of thee, O thou god An of millions of years, whose form and whose beauty of face are all-pervading in Ta-tchesert (i.e., the Underworld).[6]

From the Papyrus of Ani (sheet 19) we find:

PRAISE BE UNTO THEE, OSIRIS, lord of eternity, UN-NEFER-HERU-KHUTI whose forms are manifold, and whose attributes are majestic, PTAH-SEKER-TEM in Annu (Heliopolis), the lord of the Hidden House, the creator of Het-ka-Ptah (Memphis) and of the gods [therein], thou guide of the Underworld, whom [the gods] glorify when thou settest in the night sky of Nut. Isis embraceth thee with content, and she driveth away the fiends from the mouth of thy paths. Thou turnest thy face upon Amentet, and thou makest the earth to shine as with refined copper. Those who have lain down (i.e., the dead) rise up to look upon thee, they breathe the air and they look upon thee, they breathe the air and they look upon thy face when the disk riseth on the horizon their hearts are at peace inasmuch as they behold thee, O thou who art Eternity and Everlastingness.[7]

An address to Osiris is additionally presented in the Saite Recension in Chapter CXXVIII of *The Book of the Dead:*

HOMAGE TO THEE, O OSIRIS UN NEFER, whose word is maat, thou son of Nut, thou first-born son of Seb, thou mighty one comest forth from Nut, thou king in the city of Nifu-ur, thou Governor of Amentet, thou lord. of Abtu, thou lord of souls, thou mighty one of strength, thou lord of the Atef crown

6, 7 Ibid.

CHAPTER 20

Suten-henen, thou lord of the tomb, thou mighty one of souls
in Tattu thou lord of [sepulchral] offerings, whose festivals are
many in Tattu. The god Horus exalteth his father in every
place, and he uniteth himself unto the goddess Isis and unto
her sister Nephthys; and the god Thoth reciteth for him the
might glorifyings which are within him, and which come forth
from his mouth, and the heart of Horus is stronger than that of
all the gods. Rise up, then, O Horus, thou son of Isis, and
avenge thy father Osiris. Hail, O Osiris, I have come unto thee;
I am Horus and I have avenged thee, and I feed this day upon
the sepulchral meals of oxen and feathered fowl, and upon all
the beautiful things offered unto Osiris. Rise up, then, O
Osiris, for I have struck down for thee all thine enemies, and I
have taken vengeance upon them for thee. I am Horus upon
this beautiful day of thy fair rising in thy Soul, which exalteth
thee along with itself on this day before thy divine sovereign
princes. Hail, O Osiris, thy double (ka) hath come unto thee
and rests with thee, and thou restest therein in thy name of
Ka-Hetep. It maketh thee glorious in thy name of Khu, and it
maketh thee like unto the Morning Star in thy name of Pehu,
and it openeth for thee the ways in thy name of Ap-uat. Hail,
O Osiris, I have come unto thee, and I have set thine enemies
under thee in every place, and thy word is Maat in the presence of the gods and of the divine sovereign chiefs. Hail, O
Osiris, thou hast received thy sceptre and the place whereon
thou art to rest, and thy steps are under thee. Thou bringest
food to the gods, and thou bringest sepulchral meals unto
those who dwell in their tombs. Thou hast given thy might
unto the gods, and thou has created the Great God; thou hast
thy existence with them in their spiritual bodies, thou gather-
est thyself unto all the gods, and thou hearest the word of
Maat on the day when offerings to this god are ordered on the
festivals of Uka.[8]

In chapter CLXXXIII of *The Book of the Dead* another homage to
Osiris is given:

8   Ibid.

176

HOMAGE TO THEE, O GOVERNOR OF THOSE WHO ARE IN AMENTI, who makest mortals to be born again, who renewest thy youth, thou comest who dwellest in thy season, and who art more beautiful than, thy son Horus hath avenged thee; the rank and dignity of Tem have been conferred upon thee, O Un-nefer. Thou art raised up, O Bull of Amentet, thou art established in the body of Nut, who uniteth herself unto thee, and who cometh forth with thee. Thy heart is established upon that which supporteth it, and thy breast is as it was formerly; thy nose is firmly fixed with life and power, thou livest, and thou art renewed, and thou makest thy self young like Ra each and every day. Mighty, mighty is Osiris in victory, and he is firmly stablished with life.[9]

9   Ibid.

Nothing to fear in God;
nothing to feel in Death;
Good can be attained;
Evil can be endured

CHAPTER 21

Greek Mystery Schools

The Hellenistic age began in the Mediterranean with Alexander of Macedon's conquests. The annexed territories of Greece, Syria, Asia Minor, Egypt, Persia, Mesopotamia, and parts of India integrated with each other during the centuries after the death of Alexander the Great.

A common language, a vast world trade, Greek settlements throughout the whole "habitable earth," with Greek scholars, musicians, artists, philosophers, poets traveling ubiquitously—these were important factors in the development of a more or less uniform civilization that embraced the whole Mediterranean basin and the Near East, and whose far-flung outposts extended, eventually, from the Strait of Gibraltar to the River Indus, and from the forests of Germany and the steppes of Russia to the Sahara Desert and the Indian Ocean.

The most influential theology was that of the old Greek religion, its deities, beliefs, and conceptions. Rarely did an ancient cult ever come to an end. Instead, the old cults lived on, some of them extremely primitive, others more advanced. On the borders of civilization, as among the Celts, Germans, Getae, and Scythians, wholly barbarous rites still survived, including (as among the Druids) human sacrifice.

At the same time there was a genuine advance in religious ideas during this period, an advance to which philosophy made a considerable contribution and in which the higher cults influenced the lower (Greek cults, for example, influenced the barbarian); but chiefly, no doubt, the advance was the result of that mysterious inner source of change and development that affects all civilizations, arts, religions, and human culture generally. In some instances the change was beneficial, in others it was not; we find instances where the modifications have strengthened and purified a cult, others where religion has become a burden upon society.

The Anatolian worship of the Mother Goddess Cybele, originating at Pessinus in Phrygia, was identified with other cults of the Mother Goddess—e.g. the one at Ma in Cappadocia. Associated with the worship of Cybele was the worship of Attis (or Adonis), young consort of the aged Mother Goddess. Other and related cults, also originally associated with vegetation and the cycle of the seasons, were those of Tammuz (or Adonis: from the Semitic *Adon*, Lord), Atargatis (or Derceto the Syrian Goddess), Baal (or Bel: Master, Owner), and many others. But the greatest of all the Oriental deities came from still farther East—from Persia via Babylon, and originally from Vedic India—the sun god Mithras. This later cult gradually spread through Asia Minor and eventually arrived at Rome, and from there passed on, largely via the Roman armies, to the northern and western provinces. The cult of Mithras flourished during the third and fourth centuries—a period in which the early Christian Church was its chief competitor.

These mystery schools set the precedent for many of the concepts that were to reincarnate in different theologies throughout history and up to the present. The descent or fall and ascent of the soul; reincarnation; the cyclical view of history, and the expectation of a great world renewal, if not of a future age; the concept of a divine man; the tradition of secret, sacred wisdom from the hoary past, as transmitted by Hermes to Tat (or Thoth) and by him to the Hermetic votaries; the

Gnostic cosmogony, with a vast hierarchy of aeons extending downward from the primal essence to the lowest level of foul matter; the doctrine of Fate and of its overcoming, not by magic only or by theurgy, but by ascetic devotion and self-sacrifice, by purity of life, by knowledge, by renunciation, by fellowship with the enlightened, by love for man—and so we approach the Christian circle of ideas. Little wonder that Judaism (in Philo, for example) found itself at home in such a world—or at least in part of it—and came to be looked upon as a high philosophical religion; and that Christianity, a little later on, found a language at hand for the expression of its own highest concepts and hearts ready for the proclamation of its gospel. Increasingly, throughout the later Hellenistic age (especially after 250 B.C.) and down through the Hellenistic-Roman age to the very end of paganism, there was a widespread hunger for knowledge of the deity by a clear and incontestable revelation; a great desire for participation or sharing in the divine life, sacramentally or mystically; for release from servitude to the malevolent cosmic powers that hold humankind in leash; for cleansing from pollution and guilt, age-old and ingrained in human nature; and for the guarantee of a blessed future in the world to come or in some realm beyond this present evil one.

The Greek concepts of death and the afterlife are represented in Democritus' book *Concerning Those in Hades*, Stobaeus' *Sibyls and Seers*, Book XI of *The Odyssey* by Homer describing Odysseus' descent to Hades, and Virgil's "Vision of the Other World" in Book VI of *Aeneid*.

Plato describes in *Euthyphro*, a consolation addressed to Apollonius 41.109:

> They tell the following story of the Italian [i.e., South Italian Greek] Euthyphro. He was the son of a certain Elysius, a man of Terina, foremost of the citizens in virtue, wealth, and reputation. Euthyphro died very suddenly from some unknown cause. Then it occurred to Elysius, as it might have occurred to anyone under such circumstances, that perhaps his son had been poisoned; for Euthyphro was his only son, and heir to his vast property and wealth. Being perplexed as to how he might

181

put the matter to a test, he visited a soul oracle [psychoman-
teion, a place where the spirits of the dead are conjured up].
Having first offered a sacrifice, according to the rule, he lay
down to sleep and saw the following vision. He thought his
own dead father had come to him; and so Elysius told him the
misfortune that had happened to his son, and prayed and
begged him to help him find out what had caused his son's
death. "It is for this very purpose," replied the ghost, "that I
have come, but take from the hand of my companion what he
brings you; from that you will know the whole truth of the
event over which you are sorrowing." The person he pointed
to was a young man following him, who closely resembled
Euthyphros, and was like him in both age and stature. "Who
are you?" Elysius asked. And he replied, "I am your son's
guardian spirit," and with that he handed Elysius a little
scroll. When Elysius had unrolled it he found written within
it these three lines: "Of a truth the minds of men wander in
ignorance; Euthyphro died by a natural death, in accordance
with destiny. For it was not well that he should live, either for
him or for his parents."[1]

The Eleusinian Mystery School deals with the mother (Demeter)
and her daughter (Kore). Pluto, the god of the underworld, abducts
Kore and Demeter grieves over this loss. The following tables in the
temple of Cnidus reflect this story.

I devote to Demeter and Kore the one who said of me that I
was preparing a deadly poison for my husband. By [order of]
Demeter may he be sold [or burned] with what he possesses,
confessing all and may he find Demeter and Kore not easily
reconciled [with him], nor the gods that are with Demeter. But
let purity and freedom remain with me, rather than that I
should ever dwell with him under one roof or in any way have
dealings with him. And I likewise curse the one who has written against me or has directed it. May he find Demeter and
Kore and the gods that are with Demeter not easily reconciled,

---

1   *Plato, 1988.*

but may he and all that he possesses be burned up by [order of] Demeter.

I devote to Demeter and Kore and the gods with Demeter those who laid hands on me, beat me, and bound me, and also those who enticed me out. May they not escape, but let me be clean ...

Let him be devoted to Artemis, Demeter, Kore [and] all the gods that are with Demeter—whoever does not return to me the mantles, clothing, and [other] apparel I left behind, after I have asked for them. Let him be brought before Demeter, and if anyone else has anything of mine let him be burned [by fever? Or perhaps "sold," i.e., into slavery], confessing it. But me—let me be pure and free, and drink and eat [with others], and dwell under the same roof. I have been treated unjustly, Lady Demeter![2]

Healings were common in the great shrine of Asclepius. New methods of healing were expected to result in marvelous cures. Great physicians were even expected, like the gods, to raise the dead. Pliny decries the new methods of Asclepius (*Apleius* [ca. 40 B.C.] *Florida* 19) and the latter's raising of the dead.[3] The Emperor Vespasian was credited with miracles of healing, even with the "king's touch." Such a popular ascetic philosopher and liturgiologist as Apollonius of Tyana not only described exorcisms and instances of healing the blind, the lame, and the sick among the Indians, but was himself credited with performing similar miracles, and even with raising the dead. Even the skeptical Lucian told of incredible recoveries, like that of the vine-dresser Midas who had been bitten by a serpent while at work in the vineyard and was brought back to life by a "Babylonian, one of the so-called Chaldeans," who drove out the poison by means of a spell and by fastening to his foot a piece of stone that he broke off the tomb of a dead maiden.

---

2   Ibid.
3   W. C. K. Guthrie, *Orpheus and Greek Religion* (Princeton: Princeton University Press, 1993).

CHAPTER 21

ORPHISM

Orphism is the first religious movement in the Greek world to have a personal founder (Orpheus) and to set forth its doctrines in writing. Its origins go back to the sixth or seventh century B.C., but it enjoyed a wide revival and increased influence during the Hellenistic and Hellenistic-Roman age. New and ever profounder meanings were read into its rites and myths.

There are two distinct components of Orphism. The first is a body of traditional poetry, possibly from as early as the seventh century B.C, ascribed to a mythical singer called Orpheus and containing an account of the creation of the world and of the afterlife of the soul, its judgment and punishment for sins on earth, and its final reincarnation in another living body. The second is the way of life adopted by those who accepted the truth of these writings, such truths being regarded with as much respect as the revelations in the traditional Greek "mysteries" at Eleusis and elsewhere.

Orphic poetry represents a compendium of accounts of theogeny, cosmogony, and the nature and fate of the soul. Orpheus first appeared in Greek art and literature as a famous singer during the sixth century B.C. The tradition that Orpheus sang while Musaeus wrote down his master's songs may reflect the moment of transition from oral to written literature—which probably occurred in the second half of the seventh century B.C. and this may be the time when these songs were composed.

The poets of ancient Greece looked upon Orpheus as a singer with supernatural abilities. According to an Alexandrian poet, Orpheus soothed quarreling companions by singing to them of the creation of the world and of the dynasties of the gods. Euripides wrote of Orpheus' special connection with the underworld. A Naples bas-relief, executed at the end of the fifth century B.C., depicts his attempt to bring back his wife Eurydice from the dead. A little earlier in the same century, Polygnotus executed his famous picture of the underworld in which Orpheus was shown, lyre in hand, amidst a group of legendary musicians.

The figure of Orpheus mirrored the philosophy of ancient Greece. This theogony is an account of creation and a depiction of the fate of the soul in the underworld.

Initiation into the mysteries was supposed to give a revelation of truth that would enable men to reach the next world in a state of guilt-lessness. The following gold plates were found from Petelia and Thuri in Italy, in graves dating from the fourth or third century B.C.:

Plate from Petelia (32a)
In the house of Hades, at the left hand, you will find a spring
And, just a few steps beyond it, a single white cypress.
But take care not [to] come near the spring;
Instead you will find other cooling waters, streaming forth.
From Mnemosyne's lake—but here watchers are at hand.
Say to them: "I am a son of Earth and of starry Heaven,
[I am of heavenly descent;] this ye yourselves know.
I am languishing from thirst, and about to pass away;
    quickly then give me to drink
Cooling water from the spring, swelling from the lake of
    Mnemosyne [Memory]."
Gladly then will they give you to drink from the divine spring,
And henceforth with other heroes you will reign.

Plate from Thurii (32c)
Pure I come hither from the pure, O divine mistress of Hades,
Eucles, Eubuleus, and yet other immortal gods.
For I claim for myself to be a sprout of your blessed stem.
But the Moira compelled me, and the other undying gods,
    ... and he hurled forth the lightning and thunder.
By good fortune I have escaped the circle of burdensome care,
And to the crown of yearning have I come with swift foot.
I bury myself in the lap of the Lady who rules in Hades.
Yea with swift foot have I attained the crown of desire.
Fortunate art thou, and blessed, and wilt be no longer
    a man but god.
Like a kid have I fallen into the milk![3]

---

3 Ibid.

ORPHIC HYMNS

The following hymns were reportedly composed by Orpheus and addressed to various gods:

XVIII. To Pluto
Oh thou who dwellest in the underearthly house, thou
    mighty of soul
Amid the deep-shadowed, never-lighted fields of Tartarus,
Thou scepter-bearing Zeus of the underworld,
Thou who holdest the keys of the whole world,
Thou who vouchsafest all wealth to the generations of
    men year by year
Thou who alone holdest all sway over the world's third part—
The world, dwelling place of the immortals, solid ground
    where mankind dwells
Thou who hast set thy throne in the gloomy realm below,
In far-flung Hades, dismal, measureless, all-embracing,
    torn by tempestuous winds,
Where dark Acheron winds about the deep roots of earth;
Thou who rulest mortals by the power of death, and
    receivest all;
Great God, Wise Counselor [Eubuleus];
Thou who once didst marry the daughter of holy Demeter,
Snatching her away from the pleasant meadows
And carrying her through the sea in thy swift chariot
To the cave in Attica, in Eleusis' vale
Where stand the gates of Hades.
Thou alone art ruler of all things visible and invisible,
Inspired God, All-ruler [Pantocrator], most holy, most
    highly praised
Who dost rejoice over the worthy mystes and his sacred
    ministrations.
I invoke thee and implore thee,
Graciously come, and show thyself favorable to thy initiates!

XXIX. To Persephone
O Persephone, daughter of great Zeus,
Come, only-begotten goddess, and receive the offering
    piously dedicated unto thee—
To thee, Pluto's honored bride,
The kindly [kedne], the lifegiver;
Thou who rulest the gates of Hades in the clefts of the earth,
Executrix of punishments, the lovely-tressed, pure
    offspring of Zeus;
Mother of the Eumenides, Queen of the nether world,
Whom Zeus by a secret union begat as his daughter;
Mother of the noisy, many-formed Eubuleus,
Leader of the dance of the Hours, Light-bringer, beautiful
    in form;
Exalted, all-ruling Kore, bounteous in fruits,
Clear-shining one, horned, the one and only desired of
    all mortals;
The bringer of springtime, when thou art pleased with the
    sweet-smelling meadows,
When thou dost let thy heavenly form be seen
In the green, fruit-bearing growth of the field,
And are set free for the gathering of the mighty harvest sheaves;
Thou who alone art life and death to mortals, greatly plagued,
Persephoneial [well named]
For thou ever bringest forth [phereis] all things,
And slayest all [phoneuseis]! Hear, O blessed goddess!
Let the fruits of the earth spring forth
And grant us peace away, sound health, and a prosperous life;
Then at last, after a hale old age,
Lead us down to thy realm, O Queen,
And to Pluto, the Lord of all.[4]

---

4   Ibid.

F. Bucheler's *Carmina Latina Epigraphica No. 111* presents an inspection concerning initiates:

> But these are nothing. Thou, O pious mystes,
> Dost hide, within that secret inmost shrine
> Of thy pure heart, what holy initiates know,
> Honoring the manifold majesty of God.
> Thy spouse thou takest for fellow in thy prayer
> At every sacrifice; she truly shares
> With thee all mysteries in heaven and earth.
> Shall I recount thine honors, or thy power,
> Or those rich joys that all men long to gain?
> All these were ever fleeting, in thine eyes;
> The holy priestly fillet was thy crown.
> Belov'd, by virtue of the teaching thou
> Hast set me free from this fell lot of death!
> For pure and chaste was I when thou
> Unto the temple leddest me, and to the gods
> Devoted me their servant, guiding me,
> A full initiate in the holy rite
> As priestess of the Mother of the Gods
> And Attis; so thou honoredst me as spouse
> Through the red sacrament, the blood of bull,
> And taught me that deep threefold mystery
> Of Hecat, yea, and made me worthy e'en
> To share Demeter's blessed age-old rites.[5]

DIOGENES: A PHILOSOPHICAL TESTAMENT

This inscription on a portico beside the road near Oenoanda, in Lycia, is the philosophical legacy of an Epicurean named Diogenes, who lived ca. A.D. 200. In a world of superstition, in which the after-life was usually thought of with uneasy forebodings, the following brief summary of the teachings of philosophy with its account of the views of various schools must have brought peace of mind to many a weary traveler:

---

5   Ibid.

Having arrived by our years at the sunset of life, and expecting at any time now to depart out of the world with a glad song and a heart filled with happiness, we have decided, lest we be snatched away too soon, to offer some help to the rightly disposed.

For if even one person, or perhaps two or three or four or five or six, or any larger number you choose—but not everyone—were in trouble, O fellow mortal, and I were called upon to help them one after another, I would do everything I could to give them good advice. But now, as I have said, the majority of mankind are everywhere sick as with a pestilence, by reason of their false beliefs about things. And the number of the diseased grows steadily; for they imitate one another, and catch the illness from each other like an epidemic in a flock of sheep. Furthermore, it is only right to help those who are to come after us, since they too belong to us, though not yet born. And finally, love for mankind bids us render aid to strangers passing.

Since, therefore, the help provided in writing [or from the writings, i.e., of Epicurus] is more certain, I have decided to use this wall [literally, stoa] to set forth the medicine needed for the healing [of mankind].

Epicurus' letter to Menoeceus § 33ff stated:
Nothing to fear in God;
Nothing to feel in Death;
Good can be attained;
Evil can be endured.

SALLUSTIUS—CONCERNING THE GODS AND THE UNIVERSE

Sallustius was a Greek philosopher who reportedly lived in the fourth century A.D. He is best known for his treatise *Concerning the Gods and the Universe*, which he wrote as an introduction to religious studies. In this work Sallustius sums up the doctrinal views of that group of philosophically educated, spiritually minded pagans who were still hoping, at the end of the fourth century, to see the old religion restored:

§20 The Transmigration of Souls
If transmigration of a soul happens into a rational creature, the
soul becomes precisely that body's soul; if into an unreasoning
creature, the soul accompanies it from outside as our guardian
spirits accompany us; for a rational soul could never become
the soul of an irrational creature. The reality of transmigration
can be seen from the existence of congenital complaints (else
why are some born blind, some born paralyzed, some born
diseased in soul?) and from the fact that souls which are naturally qualified to act in the body must not, once they have left
it, remain inactive throughout time. Indeed, if souls do not
return into bodies, they must either be unlimited in number or
God must continually be making others. But there is nothing
unlimited in the universe, since in what is ordered by limit
there cannot be anything unlimited. Nor is it possible that
other souls should come into being, for everything in which
something new is produced must be imperfect, and the universe, as proceeding from what is perfect, should be perfect.

§21. The Reward of Virtue both Here and Hereafter
Souls that have lived in accordance with virtue have as the
crown of their happiness that are free from the unreasonable
element and purified from all body they are in union with the
gods and share with them the government of the whole universe. Yet, even if they attained none of these things, virtue
itself and the pleasure and honour of virtue, and the life free
from pain and from all other tyrants, would suffice to make
happy those who had chosen to live in accordance with virtue
and had proved able.[6]

---

6   Sallustius. *Sallustius*, translated by John C. Rolfe (London: Heinemann, 1931).

It is through our love
for the soul that
we can best aid
its journey to heaven

CHAPTER 22

Christian Masses

The early Christians based many of their ideas on disposal of their dead on the rituals of the Hebrews, as expanded by the teachings of Christ. It was believed that death did not result in an absolute separation of the departed from the living. The soul is not destroyed by death, but resurrected in a glorified body. Jesus taught that every human soul is both spiritual and immortal.

To the early Christians, death was a birth into eternity. This was not a time to show hopelessness and grief. Death was a form of sleep; the word "cemetery" means a sleeping place. The burial customs were rather simple and these duties were listed among the seven Corporal Works of Mercy enjoined on all Christians.

The requirements for burial were established by early canon law. A cross was placed on the breast; the hands were folded if no cross was available. Lights were set by the body and holy water and incense were applied to it at certain intervals. A coffin was not required, but the body was to be buried in consecrated ground.

The family took the responsibility for the dead. They could touch the dead since the body was sacred. This represented a major break from the Hebrew custom of not touching the body of the dead. Since the soul was thought to leave the body through the feet, the feet were stretched out. *Viaticum* (Communion) was given to the dying, lending strength for their journey to heaven. This word is Roman in origin and literally meant an allowance of money or supplies for transportation.

Other rituals included washing the body and anointing it with spices, closing the eyes and the mouth, and wrapping the departed in a linen sheet. Then the body was placed on a couch to be viewed by friends and relatives for a minimum of eight hours prior to burial.

Wakes had their origin in ancient Jewish practices that represented fears of burying a person who was still alive. This "watching" or "waking" of the dead took place for three days in an effort to prevent premature burial, which apparently was not uncommon in days past. At this time the early Christians said prayers for the dead and sang psalms in the evening. Wakes were customary in a number of cultures.

Requiem Masses had to be conducted and Holy Communion distributed before noon. The singing of psalms and hymns and the recitation of prayers and reading of the scripture characterized burials in the afternoon. A reverent and subdued atmosphere prevailed at early Christian funeral processions.

Music, partying, and noisy display were forbidden at this time. Young men carried the corpse to the gravesite as an act of mercy and were never paid for this service. The theme was a triumph over death, but with a subdued atmosphere. A special memorial for the dead was designated on the third, seventh or ninth, thirtieth or fortieth days and the anniversary of the death with Requiem Masses.

Christ said we can live forever. He died for the sins of humankind and the world has been redeemed through his death and resurrection. It is interesting to note that this concept of resurrection first appeared in *The Egyptian Book of the Dead*[1] (see chapter 20) in reference to the god Osiris.

1 Budge, 1895.

Christians are encouraged to comfort the sick and dying, as well as console the bereaved, by praying for the dead. It would be a greater sin to bury the dead twice, in the grave and in our hearts, by ignoring this concept. The soul must be kept alive by focusing on its virtues and guiding it to its eternal reward. It is through our love for the soul that we can best aid its journey to heaven.

St. Paul's entreaty for Onesiphorus is the one specific reference to an apostle praying for the dead. In 2 Timothy 1:18, we find: "May the Lord grant him to find mercy from the Lord on that day."

We must distinguish between the Christian philosophy of praying *for* the dead versus the pagan practice of praying *to* the dead.[2] It was only the martyrs and apostles that entered heaven immediately upon death. For the average person, judgment resulted in a stay in purgatory until all sins were removed. These prayers for the dead facilitated the ascension into heaven.

The Eucharist is one of the most ancient Christian practices and it represents a commemoration of the departed soul:

> Remember, Lord, those who have died and have gone before us marked with the sign of faith, especially those for whom we now pray, N. and N. May these, and all who sleep in Christ, find in your presence light, happiness, and peace (Eucharistic Prayer I).

> Remember our brothers and sisters who have gone to their rest in the hope of rising again; bring them and all the departed into the light or your presence (Eucharistic Prayer II).

> Welcome into your kingdom our departed brothers and sisters, and all who have left this world in your friendship (Eucharistic Prayer III).

> Remember those who have died in the peace of Christ and all the dead whose faith is known to you alone (Eucharistic Prayer IV).[3]

---

2 Jacques Le Goff, *The Birth of Purgatory*, trans. Arthur Goldhammer (Chicago: The University of Chicago Press, 1984), p. 45.

3 Aristides. L. J. Doyle and W. A. Jurgens (trans.), *Theological Dimensions of the Liturgy* (Collegeville, MN: The Liturgical Press, 1976), p. 337.

In Matthew 23:34, we learn that the Eucharist has as its purpose the facilitation of the soul's journey to the kingdom of heaven. Aristides of Athens, in the year A.D. 140, averred: "If one of the faithful dies, obtain salvation for him by celebrating the Eucharist and by praying next to his remains."[4]

Edmund Fortman, in his book *The Triune God: A Historical Study of the Doctrine of the Trinity*, writes, "The early Church did not seem to be very clear about where these were or how prayer would help them, but she definitely knew that prayer and the Mass could be of benefit for these faithful Christians."[5]

The Church assigned the archangel Michael with the role of protector of Christians against the devil. This is especially evident at the moment of death when he assists the soul on its journey to heaven. It was during the twelfth and thirteenth centuries that the Last Judgment dominated Christian thought. Michael is often depicted weighing the souls of the dead in a balance scale. Michael became regarded as the patron saint of the dead. This is reminiscent of the Judgment Scene in *The Egyptian Book of the Dead*, in the Papyrus of Ani[6] (see chapter 20).

The Council of Florence (1439) and the Council of Trent (1563) represent excellent sources for praying for the dead. At the Florence Council, it was stated:

> But if they die [after Penance] truly repenting in charity before making satisfaction by worthy fruits for what they have done or omitted to do, their souls are purged after death ... by the punishments of purgation and purification. The intercession of the living faithful is effective in lessening this punishment, by the sacrifice of the Mass, prayer, almsgiving, and other pious works which the faithful are wont to do.[7]

At Trent, the value of praying for the deceased was further reinforced.

---

4 Leonard J. Doyle and W. A. Jurgens, trans. City in Cyprian Vagaggini, *Theological Dimensions of the Liturgy*, (Collegeville, MN: The Liturgical Press, 1976), p. 337.

5 (Philadelphia: Westminster Publishing, 1972).

6 Budge, 1895.

7 Doyle, 1976.

There is a purgatory, and that the souls detained therein are aided by the suffrages of the faithful and chiefly by the acceptable sacrifice of the altar.[8]

The most recent council of the Catholic Church, referred to as Vatican II, met from 1962 to 1965 in Rome. During this gathering, the practice of praying for the dead was reaffirmed.

St. Odilo, the Abbot of Cluny, in 998. began what is termed today All Soul's Day. November 2 was designated as a "day of all the departed ones." Vespers were read on November 1 and then the soul bell was rung. Next, the Office of the Dead was recited and the following day was characterized by masses said for the souls in purgatory by all the priests of the monasteries.

The following are examples of prayers for the dead:

For the Dying

Jesus, savior and Lover of souls, by the memory of Your Own agonizing death on the cross, have mercy upon all the dying. At every instant, sweet Jesus, some poor souls are trembling on the threshold of eternity, about to appear before Your awful judgement. Have mercy on them all, with a most tender mercy, at this the hour of their greatest need.

Remember dear Jesus, the awful price which You have paid for their redemption. Remember the anguish of Your agony in the Garden, the bloody sweat with which You bedewed the ground, the pang of Your betrayal, the insolence and cruelty of Your executions, the mocker of Your trial, the torture of Your scourging, the weariness and suffering of your Way of the Cross! Oh, by these holy memories, help the souls of the dying!

Remember, most good and merciful Jesus, the anguish of Your crucifixion, the bitterness of Your dereliction, Your thirst and sufferings, and Your agonizing death, and help and heal the souls of the departing. Give them strength, dear Lord, at the

---

8 Ibid.

last hour. Give them love and sorrow. Sustain them by your holy graces; deliver them from the attacks of the enemy. We ask it of You through the intercession of the Blessed Virgin, Your Mother, and of all Your angels and saints. Amen.[9]

—Rev. Edward Garesche, S.J.

For a Happy Death and for a Happy End

Divine Jesus, mighty Savior, Conqueror of death and sin, the time is swiftly approaching when we shall each one be summoned to pass through the dark doors of death into Your kingdom of eternity. May the prayers of Your own Sacred Heart, of the Immaculate Heart of Your Virgin Mother, and of all the angels and the saints in heaven and the just on earth, together with the mighty efficacy of all Holy Masses rise up forever in petition for us for a holy and happy death. Amen.

Remind us frequently, dear Lord, to pray for the dying and for our own happy death. Accept all our thoughts and the words and actions, in union with Your Sacred Heart and with the Immaculate Heart of Your holy Mother, in petition for this great boon. May our death and that of each one for whom we are bound or wish especially to pray, be serene and tranquil, guarded round by all the holy angels, protected by our patron saints. May our hearts at that supreme moment be full of the pure love of You, may our souls be clean from every stain. Make our faith, then, perfect and untroubled, our hope most bright and strong and our love pure and mighty, when we go forth to meet You, our Saviours and our Judge. Multiply, great Lord at that tremendous moment. Your effective graces. Thus may we praise You, sweet Jesus, and thank You throughout all ages of eternity, where You live and reign, with the Father and the Holy Ghost, one Eternal God, the peace and joy of all the blessed, world without end. Amen.[10]

—Rev. Edward Garesche, S.J.

9, 10   Rev. Edward F. Garesche. *Moments with God* (Bruce Publishing Co., Milwaukee, 1942).

For All the Deceased

By Thy resurrection from the dead, O Christ, death no longer hath dominion over those who die in holiness. So, we beseech Thee, give rest to Thy servants in Thy sanctuary and in Abraham's bosom. Grant it to those, who from Adam until now have adored Thee with purity, to our fathers and brothers, to our kinsmen and friends, to all men who have lived by faith and passed on their road to Thee, by a thousand ways, and in all conditions, and make them worthy of the heavenly kingdom.[11]

Prayer to the Trinity for Final Perseverance

Father, Son and Holy Ghost, Eternal Trinity, I beg of You by the life, passion and death of Jesus Christ, and by the merits of the Blessed Virgin and of all the angels and saints, give to me the grace of final perseverance, of a happy death and a blessed eternity. May the last moments of my life, my God, be the best and holiest. Provide for me a time of repentance and atonement, the grace to be fortified at my death with Your holy sacraments, protection from yielding to temptation in my last hour, and the grace of loving and serving You even to the end of my life. I wish this prayer to be the constant intention of all my thoughts and words and actions, of all Masses and Communions, of all the merits that I am able to gain in Your sight, during all the days of my life. Divine Father, You have created me, please have pity on me at the moment of my death. Divine Son, You have redeemed me, please have mercy on me at my last hour. Holy Spirit, You have sanctified me, please keep me holy at the last. And you, my blessed Mother, and all you saints and angels of God, I rely on you all to aid me at my last hour, and to bring me safe, by your prayers, through the darkness of death, to the light and glory of your eternal home. Amen.[12]

—Rev. Edward Garesche, S.J.

11, 12 Ibid.

For a Happy Death

O my dear Lord Jesus Christ, I do most humbly beseech Thee by those bitter pains Thou didst suffer for us in Thy cruel Passion, particularly in that hour wherein Thy divine Soul passed forth from Thy blessed Body, that Thou wouldst take pity on our souls in their last agony and passage to Eternity. And do Thou, O compassionate Virgin Mother, remember how thou didst sadly stand by thy be loved Son dying on the Cross; by thy grief and thy son's death assist us at our death and conduct us to a happy eternity. Amen.[13]

—Rev. John P. O'Connell

Prayer for the Poor Souls

O God the light of those who live, the hope of those who die, the salvation of all who trust in Thee: mercifully grant that the souls of Thy servants and handmaidens being freed from the chains of our mortal nature, may by the intercession of Blessed Mary, ever a Virgin, rejoice together with Thy saints in everlasting light. Amen.[14]

—The Dominican Missal

For the Dead

Be mindful, O Lord, of Thy servants who on departing this life were found unfit to enter into Thy joy, and are therefore now being prepared by suffering for that final beatitude. Grant that the claims of Thy justice may be satisfied, and the debts of these helpless sinners be fully paid for their loving Lord and Master, Jesus Christ Thy son, the one Mediator of all mankind. Amen.[15]

—Rev. John P. O'Connell

---

13 Rev. John P. O'Connell and Jex Martin, ed. *The Prayer Book* (Chicago: The Catholic Press, 1954), p. 140.

14 Rev. Edward F. Garesche. *Dominican Missal.*

15 O'Connell, p. 147.

The *Dies Irae* was used as a Requiem Mass. This poem, reportedly composed by the Franciscan Thomas of Celano in the thirteenth century, has been set to music by various noted composers.

Dies Irae

That day of wrath, that dreadful day,
Shall heaven and earth in ashes lay,
As David and the Sybil say.
What horror must invade the mind
When the approaching Judge shall find
And sift the deeds of all mankind!
The mighty trumpet's wondrous tone
Shall rend each tomb's sepulchral stone
And summon all before the Throne.
Now death and nature with surprise
Behold the trembling sinners rise
to meet the Judge's searching eyes.
Then shall with universal dread
The book of Consciences be read
To judge the lives of all the dead.
For now before the Judge severe
All hidden things must plain appear;
No crime can pass unpunished here.
Oh what shall I, so guilty, plead?
And who for me will intercede?
When even Saints shall comfort need?
O King of dreadful majesty!
Grace and mercy You grant free;
As Fount of Kindness, save me!
Recall, dear Jesus, for my sake
You did our suffering nature take.
Then do not now my soul forsake!
In weariness You sought for me,

CHAPTER 22

And suffering upon the tree!
Let not in vain such labor be.
O Judge of justice, hear, I pray,
For pity take my sins away
Before the dreadful reckoning day.
your gracious face, O Lord, I see;
Deep shame and grief are on my cheek;
In sighs and tears my sorrows speak.
You Who did Mary's guilt unbind,
And mercy for the robber find,
Have filled with hope my anxious mind.
How worthless are my prayers, I know.
Yet, Lord, forbid that I should go
Into the fires of endless woe.
Divorced from the accursed band,
O make me with Your sheep to stand,
A child of grace, at Your right Hand.
When the doomed no more can flee
From the flames of misery
With the chosen call me.
Before You, humbled, Lord, I lie.
My heart like ashes, crushed and dry.
Assist me when I die.
Full of tears and full of dread
Is that day that day that wakes the dead.
Calling all, with solemn blast
To be judged for all their past.
Lord have mercy, Jesus blest,
Grant them all Your light and Rest.
Amen.[16]

---

16 Franciscan Thomas of Celano, translated by Ruby Spine (Sag Harbor, NY: Permanent Press, 1990).

200

...the dying are attended
during the passage
from one world to another
by heavenly watchers

CHAPTER 23

Emanuel Swedenborg on Death

This Biblical scholar, scientist, and mystic studied mathematics and natural science. Swedenborg (1688–1772) was trained in Newtonian physics and developed a modern scientific outlook in his day. His many writings are characterized by great scholarship and by a fervent search for a synthesis of ancient wisdom and modern experience, empirical science, rationalistic philosophy, and Christian revelation.

His philosophy was characterized by the idea of coming into existence by motion from the Infinite. These connections between the infinite and finite world are interpreted as fundamentals of nature. This original motion is a form of consciousness and not a mechanical motion. Swedenborg contributed greatly to conscious dying by providing a glimpse into the afterlife. Even though most of his data represents unconscious dying (see chapter 2), his influence is still felt today.

In his physiological research, Swedenborg started with the study of the blood, which in its relation to the organization of the human body corresponds in some important ways to the role of the mathematical point as a nexus between the spiritual and the physical worlds. Swedenborg distinguished several degrees of purity in the

blood, with the highest degree corresponding to the Cartesian spiritu-
ous fluid. This fluid functions both as a concrete communication line
between soul and body and as an asbstract principle, a formative force
of the body (vis formatrix). Swedenborg combined this concept of life
force with Aristotle's concept of form and developed a teleological system very much like Leibniz's monadology.

Spirits, according to this eighteenth-century mystic, live in cities
where they have an active social life with social functions (even marriage) corresponding to earthly conditions. The relegation of spirits to
heaven or hell from the intervening spiritual world depends on the
spirits themselves, since their utmost desire (amor regnans) leads them
into suitable company.

He states in the *Principia* the difficulty in attaining knowledge of
the soul:

> In respect to the soul and its various faculties, I do not con-
> ceive it possible that they can be explained or comprehended
> by any of the known laws of motion; such indeed is our pre-
> sent state of ignorance, that we know not whether the motions
> by which the soul operates on the organs of the body be such
> as to be reducible to any rule or law, either similar or dissimi-
> lar to those of mechanics (Part I, Chapter I).[1]

With the aid of certain philosophical doctrines and the study of
anatomy, Swedenborg attempts to unravel the mysteries of life:

> I am strongly persuaded that the essence and nature of the soul,
> its influx into the body, and the reciprocal action of the body,
> can never come to demonstration, without these doctrines [he
> is referring to his Doctrine of Order, and Science of Universals],
> combined with a knowledge of anatomy, pathology, and psy-
> chology; nay, even of physics, and especially of the auras of the
> world; and that unless our labours take this direction and
> mount from phenomena thus, we shall in every new age have
> to build new systems, which in their turn will tumble to the
> ground, without the possibility of being rebuilt.

1–18 Swedenborg, 1865. Reprinted with permission of The Swedenborg Foundation.

This, and no other, is the reason that, with diligent study and intense application, I have investigated the anatomy of the body [in all its parts]. In doing this, I may perhaps have gone beyond the ordinary limits of inquiry, so that but few of my readers may be able distinctly to understand me. But thus far I have felt bound to venture, for I have resolved, cost what it may, to trace out the nature of the human soul (*The Economy of the Animal Kingdom*, Part II, Nos. 213 and 214).[2]

His frustration with this study was noted:

I could not but think with mankind in general, that all our knowledge of it was to be attempted either by a bare reasoning philosophy, or more immediately by the anatomy of the human body. But on making the attempt, I found myself as far from my object as ever; for no sooner did I seem to have mastered the subject, than I found it again eluding my grasp, though it never absolutely disappeared from my view....Thus did I seem to see, and yet not to see, the very object, with the desire of knowing which I was never at rest. But at length I awoke as from a deep sleep, when I discovered, that nothing is further removed from the human understanding than what at the same time is really present to it; and that nothing is more present to it than what is universal, prior, and superior; since this enters into every particular, and into everything posterior and inferior. What is more omnipresent than the Deity,—in Him we live and are, and move,—and yet what is more remote from the sphere of the understanding? (*The Economy of the Animal Kingdom*, Part II. No. 208).[3]

In *Heaven and Hell*, No. 130, we read, in reference to the spiritual light in the Heavens:

I was elevated into that light interiorly by degrees, and in proportion as I was elevated, my understanding was enlightened, till I was at length enabled to perceive things which I did not perceive before, and, finally, such things as I could not even comprehend by thought from natural light.[4]

CHAPTER 23

Swedenborg comments on life after death in this section from *Arcana Coelestia* (No. 70):

> That I might know that man lives after death, it has been granted me to speak and converse with several persons with whom I had been acquainted during their life in the body, and this not merely for a day or a week, but for months, and in some instances for nearly a year, as I had been used to do here on earth. They were greatly surprised that they themselves, during their life in the body, had lived, and that many others still live, in such a state of unbelief concerning a future life, when nevertheless there intervenes but the space of a few days between the decease of the body and their entrance into another world,—for death is a continuation of life.[5]

It is his own mystical out-of-body experiences that are the source of Swedenborg's philosophies:

> The dying, he tells us, are attended during the passage from one world to another by heavenly as well as earthly watchers. Angels from the celestial, or highest, heaven first minister to the passing soul, and keep the mind as far as possible in the pious and holy thoughts which are usually associated with the death-bed. The subject is at this time semi-conscious, and scarcely notices the presence of his angelic ministrants; who themselves are silent, and communicate their thoughts by a subtle influence.[6]

The recently departed are approached by the "holy ones," but find this unendurable due to the former's low level of spiritual development. Angels replace these holy ones and instruct the departed in Divine knowledge. They, in turn, withdraw if their presence is shown to be distasteful:

> When the soul thus separates himself, he is received by good spirits, who likewise do him all kind offices whilst he is in consort with them. If, however, his life in the world was such that he cannot remain associated with the good, he seeks to be disunited from them also, and this separation is repeated again

and again, until he associates himself with those whose state entirely agrees with that of his former life in the world, among whom he finds, as it were, his own life. They then, wonderful to relate, live together a life of similar quality to that which had constituted their ruling delight when in the body. On returning into this life, which appears to them as a new commencement of existence, some after a longer and others after a shorter space of time are carried thence towards hell; whilst such as have been principled in faith towards the Lord, are led by degrees from this new beginning of life to heaven (*Arcana Coelestia*, No. 316).[7]

Man appears to be his own judge and chooses his own associates. This inspirational concept of anyone, saint or sinner, given the opportunity to enter heaven is a key component to Swedenborg's approach to eternity.

It is pointed out that the initiated is unaware that he has died, since this new world is not very different from the physical plane. Many souls flatly refuse to believe that they have died. They have bodies, meet congenial companions, and note objects around them similar to what they were accustomed to while on Earth. They enjoy a real, substantial existence, instead of living in a disembodied condition, as, before they entered their new stage of life, they probably anticipated they would.

He points out the organized forms of spirits as follows:

Care should be taken not to give credence to the erroneous opinion that spirits do not possess far more exquisite sensations than during the life of the body, for I have been convinced to the contrary by experience repeated thousands of times....Spirits not only possess the faculty of sight, they live in such great light that the mid-day light of this world can scarcely be compared to it....They enjoy the power of hearing also, and that in so exquisite a degree as which, in my almost constant conversations with them, now for some years, I have had repeated opportunity of being convinced. The nature of their speech, and the sense of smell they also possess, will, by the Divine mercy of the Lord, be considered hereafter. They have, besides, a most exquisite sense of touch, whence come the pains and torments endured in hell; for all sensations have relation to the touch, of which they are merely diversities and varieties. Their desires and affections, moreover, are incomparably stronger than those possessed during the life of the body....Men think, also, after death, far more perspicuously and distinctly than during their previous life; for in a spiritual state of being, more is involved in one idea than in a thousand whilst in the natural life....In a word, man loses nothing by death, but is still a man in all respects, although more perfect than when in the body (*Arcana Coelestia*, No. 322).[8]

It should be noted that *The Tibetan Book of the Dead* (see chapter 19) also discussed the highly developed sense of hearing in the bardo state. Man, according to Swedenborg, brings with him to the after-life his thoughts, prejudices, and beliefs. These erroneous ideas need to be corrected.

This is done in the most effective and thorough way by allowing the soul to test experimentally their own ideals of bliss. In the introduction to *Conjugal Love*, we have a most interesting description of such experiences:

We are told of spirits who had looked forward to constant social intercourse with the wisest and best as their ideal of happiness, and who were therefore placed in a mansion where they might meet with such; but in a few days they grew weary of talk and begged to be let out, which was permitted after they had become thoroughly convinced of the error of their preconceptions, and had been instructed as to the true nature of heavenly joy. Others sought satisfaction in feasting with the patriarchs and apostles, and were granted the semblance of such delight, but were quickly sated. Others regard heaven as a place of perpetual worship, "where congregations ne'er break up, and Sabbaths have no end." Such were permitted to enter a temple and join in the worship there proceeding. At first they were in ecstasies; but after a long period of devotion, their fervor began to wane,—some nodded and slept, others yawned, or cried out to be released, and all were wearied with excess of pious effort. Those who had looked forward to the enjoyment of heavenly dignities, were permitted to assume such, but found no lasting satisfaction in them. All were instructed that heavenly joy is the delight of doing something that is of use to one's self and others; and the delight of use derives its essence from love and its existence from wisdom. The delight of use, originating in love through wisdom, is either side. Here the man is his own judge and his own witness; his scroll of life (Akashic records) is unrolled before him, and all his states and experiences recalled; the good that he has done for the love of goodness is confirmed as his own, while works done from the desire for merit or applause are cast aside as dross; evil that has been done and repented of is again brought to mind, to be spurned and blotted out, if repentance has been genuine; while misdeeds that have been done from the love of evil are recalled with a sense of delight, and become confirmed as part of his nature.

Souls now are given the opportunity to acquire the truth and rid themselves of erroneous beliefs. They are instructed in these doctrines by angels who present these ultimate truths in a manner compatible with the soul's level of understanding.[9]

"The Lord casts no one into hell" (*Heaven and Hell*, No. 545) said Swedenborg. He further points out that no one remains in hell who wishes to leave, but stays there because of congenial association.[10]

We are told that evil spirits are sometimes granted their desire to enter heaven, but they immediately cast themselves down headlong, unable to endure its atmosphere of purity. Another striking statement of Swedenborg's is that men are not punished for their misdeeds done in the body, but only for continuance in ill-doing. Nor are they punished for evil actions done with good, though mistaken, intention; still less for hereditary evil, except in so far as they have made it their own.

There is no vindictiveness to this Divine punishment. Divine punishment, in effect, does not exist. Evil punishes itself.

The Lord never sends any one into hell, but is desirous to bring all out of hell; still less does he induce torment; but since the evil spirit rushes into it himself, the Lord turns all punishment and tormentor to some good and use (*Arcana Coelestia*, No. 696).[11]

When the wicked are punished, there are always angels present to regulate its degree, and alleviate the pains of the sufferers (No. 967).[12]

Both heaven and hell are ruled by the strictest principles of Divine order. The government of heaven is the natural outcome of the spirit of order that reigns within all: in hell there is necessary coercion and restraint, though liberty is granted so far as it is not abused.

Heaven is divided broadly into three divisions, corresponding to the three degrees of the human mind, the celestial, the spiritual, and the natural; and in each of these heavens there is a further classification in societies, according to the specific characteristics of the inhabitants. There is a triple division also in the hells, and a similar subdivision into infernal associations. In the heavenly societies there is subordination of one to another; there are rulers and leaders and teachers; but there is nothing of the love of place and power that marks earthly governments.

The whole of heaven appears before the Lord as one man. This is a reflection of the harmonious working of this society to the general welfare. Every angel, and every society, has a function in his body politic corresponding to some particular organ or constituent of the human body. Those in special intelligence belong to the head, those in whom love is the ruling principle form the heart, the active spirits are the hands, the critical represent the kidneys, and so on with every detail. Even the skin, hair, and nails have their correlatives.

This "Grand Man" or *Maximus Homo* doctrine is greatly misunderstood. We must detach our minds from space and time to comprehend any spiritual truth, according to Swedenborg. We are not to regard the Grand Man, therefore, as an immense shape, into whose bodily form are packed away myriads of other human beings; but as representing in its totality the perfection of human qualities. As, in this world, no one man can embody all the possibilities of the race, and each has his own place in the general economy; so in the higher stage of existence every individual is complementary to all the rest, and the full MAN is only seen in the great whole. Hell, it may be added, is, in its totality, a hideous and inhuman monster.

Life in heaven, as we have seen, is not a monotonous round of religious exercises, but a scene of busy activity. Since useful service is the ground of heavenly happiness, it follows that there must be occupations in heaven. Every faculty of the mind will find employment, and idleness is not permitted even in hell. There those who are unwilling are compelled to labor, and only receive food as they perform some service.

The occupations of the angels differ from earthly employments, inasmuch as spiritual beings have not to labor for "the meat which perisheth," nor for necessary shelter and clothing, these things being provided for them freely; nevertheless, they find abundant means of employment.

> In heaven there are governments, offices, higher and lower courts of justice, arts, and handicrafts (*Conjugal Love*, No. 207).[13]

Heavenly architecture surpasses in beauty and dignity the finest efforts of human builders.

> Such is the architecture of heaven that one might say it is very art itself there; nor is this to be wondered at, because that art itself is from heaven (*Heaven and Hell*, No. 185).[14]

Heavenly architecture, however, is not the work of the angels themselves, but takes form, like their other surroundings, from their mental states. That there are constructive arts of various kinds, demanding conscious effort, we gather from several statements. In one place we read of a beautiful vase, which some spirits had made in honour of the Lord; in another, of "pieces of embroidery and knitting, the work of their own hands," which some heavenly maidens presented to three novitiate spirits; and of "scribes, who were writing out copies of the writings of the wise ones of the city," which the same spirits inspected, and "wondered to see them so neat and elegant." These spirits also "were taken to see the wonderful works that are done in a spiritual manner by the artificers" (*Conjugal Love*, No. 207).[15]

Angels of every society are sent to men, that they may safe-guard them, and withdraw them from evil affections and consequent evil thoughts, and inspire them with good affections, so far as they are willing to receive them from freedom (*Heaven and Hell*, No. 391).[16]

Heaven is by no means a place or condition of languorous ease.

Eternal rest is not idleness; for idleness occasions a languor, listlessness, stupor, and drowsiness of the mind and thence of the whole body; and these things are death and not life, still less eternal life in which the angels of heaven are (*Conjugal Love*, No. 207).[17]

A question on many minds is that of the relation of the sexes in the other life. It is commonly thought that the spiritual existence will be sexless, because Jesus declared that in heaven there is neither marrying nor giving in marriage, but that all will be "as the angels of God." Swedenborg is able, from actual experience, to inform us that sex is persistent, because it is in essence spiritual. There is the male soul and the female soul, and MAN is a conjunction of the two. Hence when married partners are truly united in this world, they will continue the same union in the next; if married life has not been the case here, or an unsuitable connection has been formed, congenial consorts will be found hereafter by all who so desire. With truly united pairs, the death of one does not mean separation, except as to conscious presence, for:

The spirit of the deceased continually dwells together with the spirit of the survivor, and this even to the death of the latter, when they again meet and are reunited, and love each other more tenderly than before (*Conjugal Love*, No. 321).[18]

All married partners meet in the other world and dwell together for a time; but if their natures are discordant they ultimately part and know each other no more. In heaven, needless to say, there is no decrepitude. As men and women advance in life there, instead of becoming feeble and incapable, their powers increase and develop.

...death is merely a transition
from one lifetime
and dimension
to the next

CHAPTER 24

Theosophy on Death

The Theosophical Society was founded by Madame H. P. Blavatsky in New York City on November 17, 1875. This organization, which formed the basis of American Spiritualism, originated with ascended masters in India, according to Madame Blavatsky, C. W. Leadbeater, and Annie Besant, who reportedly channeled these Indian adepts and wrote several detailed texts on their beliefs. More recently, Alice Bailey's Arcane School in New York was based on teachings channeled through the Tibetan Master Dj Whal Khul. Bailey made her transition in 1949.

According to the Theosophists, the world experienced alternating periods of "cosmic sleep" known as *manvantaras* and *pralayas*. *Monads* were elementary individual souls awakened during the manvantara phase. The previous rest periods constituted the pralaya circle.

Monads acquire the ability to become creators of matter themselves. Eventually they will design the next world or universe they inhabit. This growth is a gradual one, beginning with several mineral lives, then plant phases, followed by the lower animal existences, and finally human incarnations.

A monad begins as a spiritual being. Their physical existences represent a lowered state of awareness. The ultimate goal is to return to this perfect level of energy. Once the monad has reached the level of the human experience, humanity continues this evolution by taking responsibility for its progress.

During the rest periods, or pralaya, planets function as breeding stations for the next evolutionary step. Thus, reincarnation involves a combination of manvantara and pralaya cycles of physical and spiritual lives.

Theosophists believe there are five driving forces that result in rebirth:

- Desire for external impressions to reinforce self-awareness.

- The attraction of the earth.

- Karma.

- Desire for self-expression in the material world (trishna).

- Attachment to material objects and physical conditions.

Karma is thus a natural law. We forget our original spiritual nature when we are overinvolved with our ego or obsessed with materialism. The number of lifetimes necessary to achieve this perfection is considerable. According to Sinnett, we have lived approximately 800 separate lifetimes. Spiritual growth and eventual perfection of the soul prepare us to attain Nirvana. It is our consciousness or soul that is eternal and paramount in this system.

The most significant obstacle to overcome in karma is the overinvolvement of the monad with the material world. Once the human state is attained, the monad is totally responsible for its actions. Thus, theosophy views the cycle of rebirth more as a planned development, rather than the continuous suffering of classic Hinduism. Included in this global plan are ample opportunities for development.

Theosophy talks about the Higher Self, the monad itself, and the unifying principle throughout the karmic cycle and the lower self. The latter is a projection of the Higher Self in its actual form, which is different in each life. The cord connecting the Higher Self to the lower self becomes thinner as man forgets his spiritual purpose. The lower self has a semi-independent consciousness that is connected to the physical body. This relationship between the Higher Self and lower self is strengthened by initiation.

There are three components to the Higher Self. They are the Atma, Buddhi, and Manas. The manas are also referred to as the causal body. The lower self is the astral soul and enters the astral field of Kamaloka upon the death of the physical body. Indestructible elements, known as "permanent atoms," make up the physical, astral, mental, and etheric bodies. Along with the aura, these permanent atoms register the experiences of each lifetime.

A Buddhic web of life extends from the Higher Self into the etheric body and from there it manifests itself, eventually, into the physical body. These life threads (the silver cord) withdraw at death and wrap themselves around a core in the heart, taking the shape of a purple and gold flame. Here they migrate to the third cerebral cavity and, along with the permanent atoms, leave the body through the top of the head.

It is at this time that the dying person receives a panoramic review of his life. The consciousness of the lower self decays with the physical death of the body. This is why it is impossible for an individual to recall past lives without contacting the Higher Self.

The fate of the astral-etheric part of the lower self is *Kamaloka*, the astral field surrounding the earth. The soul can now indulge in any desires without fear of retribution. The spent desires remain as skandhas or astral elements, and will return in the succeeding incarnation. The permanent atoms withdraw into the mental body.

It is these skandhas (astral-etheric or etheric-physical) that are the carriers of karma. For example, a soul with a compulsive gambling problem would reincarnate with a gambling tendency. However, this would not necessarily result in a return of this affliction. The soul always has free will to grow and resist former vices.

The Higher Self falls asleep at the end of the Kamaloka tenure and re-awakens in *Devachan*. This is the world of thoughts. It is free of causes and consists only of effects. Indulging in one's thoughts is the only action in this dimension. This world is one of self-created illusions. The soul can acquire new knowledge here, along with higher aspirations. The greater the depository of thoughts and wisdom in the previous life, the longer the stay in Devachen. The mental body is discarded after the soul leaves Devachen and it arrives in Manas, the Higher Self component, housed in the causal body.

A golden thread of Buddhic matter signifies the return to a new incarnation. The permanent atoms of the Higher Self accompany this substance and bring all remaining skandhas left behind on the other lower planes.

The condition of the permanent atoms and accompanying skandas determine the condition of the new life. There are four additional factors that affect the new life. These are:

- The evolutionary learning potential of the new life.

- Relations with other people who have been born or are going to be born.

- Free will, personal preference and insistence (especially of advanced egos).

- Special missions that have been accepted.

The four or seven Lipika or "Lords of Karma" manage the process of reincarnation. These Lipika are cosmic administrators that register all actions and experiences in the akashic records and parcel out karmic tests. The Lipika function as an "etheric double" of the physical body and govern the growth of the body until the seventh year. A soul is not fully incarnated until it reaches the age of twenty-one.

C. W. Leadbeater proposed a classification of the length of time between incarnations. His data follows:

- 1,500 to 2,300 years: mature, advanced souls; initiates.

- 700 to 1,200 years: those who are going along or nearing the path of initiation; of these, about 5 years are spent in Kamaloka and up to 50 years at the Manas plane.

- 600 to 1,000 years: upper class; 20 to 25 years in Kamaloka, short stay in Manas.

- About 500 years: upper-middle class; 25 years in Kamaloka, no sojourn in Manas.

- 200 to 300 years: lower-middle class; 40 years in Kamaloka. 100 to 200 years: qualified workers; 40 years in Kamaloka. 60 to 100 years: non-qualified laborers; 40 to 50 years in Kamaloka.

- 40 to 50 years: good-for-nothings and drunks, only in Kamaloka.

- About 5 years: the lowest class; only in the lower part of Kamaloka or earth-bound, vegetative.

According to theosophists, all of our behavior both expresses our past lives and helps shape our future incarnations. They absolutely affirm the karmic universal law of cause and effect. A soul occasionally fails to acknowledge this principle due to maya, the illusion created by long intervals between cause and effect.

Karma has three levels:

- as natural law, without providence or release.

- as reward or punishment.

- as guidance, compensation, evolution, and healing.

Thus, it is our thoughts, feelings, and actions that follow us into our new lives. Cruelty in one life can lead to insanity in the next. Astral acts may also affect life on the physical plane. Undeserved accidents may be subtracted from one's karmic debt due to actions on the other planes. Other examples include miraculous rescues and significant guidance from other souls in times of need.

Theosophists feel that misdeeds are punished and positive actions are always rewarded. The greater the misdeed, the greater the punishment. A soul may suffer in as many as seven lifetimes for their previous actions.

A murderer may not be murdered in his or her next life. They may have to save the life of the victim at the cost of their own as a form of redemption. Another solution could be life-long service and devotion to others. A worthy person experiencing "bad luck" and the good fortune of an unworthy soul are examples of karmic retribution and reward.

It is part of the theosophists' view that the soul has free will and can always be helped. They do not accept the concept of predestination, for this would make karma meaningless. One is freed *by* karma, not *from* karma. There is also group karma, institutional karma, and national karma.

Our sincerity and openness to experiences foster our progress in our soul's growth. Karma and its subset of reincarnation are merely tools to achieve liberation from the cycle of birth and death. These spiritual doctrines have been presented to us by the Masters. They inform us that we attain perfection in the seventh life, following our initial steps toward spiritual development.

By helping others in their spiritual path we can remove karmic debts. It is our intentions, more so than our actions, that matter most. It is the more spiritually evolved soul that is naturally attracted to theosophic doctrines. One can only grow with an open mind and a good heart. Death is merely a transition from one lifetime and dimension to the next. We can make this a peaceful transition through the application of conscious dying techniques.

CONCLUSION

E lizabeth Kübler-Ross, author of the thanatology classic *On Death and Dying*, stated that:

> Death is simply a shedding of the physical body, like the butterfly coming out of a cocoon. It is a transition into a higher state of consciousness, where you continue to perceive, to understand, to laugh, to be able to grow, and the only thing you lose is something that you don't need anymore, and that is your physical body.[1]

Socrates is quoted by Plato to have said just before drinking the hemlock poison:

> To fear death, gentlemen, is nothing other than to think oneself wise when one is not; for it is to think one knows what one does not know. No man knows whether death may not even turn out to be the greater of blessings for a human being, and yet people fear it as if they knew for certain that it is the greatest of evils.[2]

The implication here is that death challenges us to seek life's meaning. This is nature's way of urging us to discover our true real

---

1   Kübler-Ross, 1969.
2   *Euthyphro.*

self—beyond that of the material world. Death can be our best friend. It helps us to become aware of the other worlds that are denied to us on the physical plane. Death actually assists us in finding genuine happiness.

Skeptics still scoff and ridicule such notions. They declare there can be no consciousness after the physical body dies. The Universe is comprised exclusively of material realities, and without the physical organism there can be no mind, no consciousness, and certainly no life after death. Near-death experiences are but hallucinations caused by reasons that may be psychological, pharmacological, or neurological. It may be impossible for such a thing as objective proof to ever actually exist in matters of the mind and spirit.

It may be argued that nobody who has not died can talk about death with authority; and since nobody apparently has ever returned from death, how can anybody know what death is, or what happens after it?

The Tibetan will declare there is not one person, indeed, not one living being, that has not returned from death. In fact, we all have died many deaths before we came into this incarnation. What we call birth is merely the reverse side of death, like one of the two sides of a coin, or like a door that we call "entrance" from outside and "exit" from inside a room.

People in the West disbelieve in rebirth because they cannot remember their past lives and deaths. Nobody remembers their birth, but the average person does not doubt their own presence in their current life. It is this dependence on the ego (conscious mind proper) and not their use of the subconscious that is the problem.

I have conducted well over 33,000 individual past life regressions and future life progressions on over 11,000 individual patients. I can attest to the relative ease with which anyone with a little assistance from hypnosis can access their akashic records and tap into these lifetimes.

Karma is simply cause and effect. It is totally just. One might describe it as a practical code of ethics. You are in control of your karma. Every soul plays the part of judge and jury. You can only fool yourself temporarily. Karma teaches you that you have only yourself to blame or credit for your life. Do not look to somebody else as a scapegoat.

Unconscious dying carries with it an unforgettable experience of forgetfulness and an ego-shattering disintegration which for the inexperienced voyager can be very unsettling, destroying any consciousness connection from one lifetime to another.

Conscious dying, on the other hand, opens up a wonderful and more enlightening universe to us all. We will now know many more of the secrets of life and the true meanings of existence. We will become more adept at learning more of the great spiritual lessons of the universe.

Some of you may still have strong feelings of disbelief, skepticism, and mistrust. Others may gain additional support for their beliefs and hope for the future from reading this book. My hope is that you keep your mind open. It is not hypnotherapists who heal, it is you who have the ultimate responsibility. Conscious dying allows you to expand and explore your awareness and eliminate fear, anxiety, depression, and other negative tendencies, as well as the fear of death. Hypnotherapy is neither magic nor a panacea—it is a way to help shape the future. By creating your own reality with the knowledge from your subconscious and superconscious minds, you can positively affect your present and future lives. Most importantly, conscious dying can eliminate the need to come back at all.

We sometimes forget that there is a God. God doesn't punish us— we punish ourselves. The soul always has free will. We can choose to do good or evil, right or wrong. We choose our future lives. Who would choose to kill, rape, steal, or cheat if he or she realized the karmic implications? Learning to use these principles of conscious dying to better ourselves, we are bettering the future for us all. The universe is connected by a linkage of the consciousness of all souls.

This entire process will end when you fulfill your karma. When you learn all the lessons you have to learn and show kindness and unselfish love to all those with whom you come into contact, the cycle will end. When it ends, you will go beyond the soul plane to the higher planes and, eventually, to God. Karma is merely a process of evolution, of achieving greater levels of perfection. It gives life. Conscious dying merely shortens this process.

A recent study shows that a combination of talk therapy and drugs is not significantly more effective than psychotherapy alone. This result is contrary to the conventional wisdom in medicine and the mental health system today. The researchers noted that the overuse of antide-pressants was most likely due to aggressive marketing campaigns con-ducted by drug companies. Superimposed upon this is the standard practice in the insurance industry of paying more for the use of drugs than for therapy itself.

My purpose in reporting this is to further illustrate the illusion of the physical world. Seeking salvation through drugs, or any other external approach, will only lead to unconscious dying and all of its accompanying inhibitions to the soul's liberation.

Learn about yourself. Your consciousness will give you the appro-priate answers to immortality. There is no definition of what constitutes a good death. To die at a young age in ancient Greece was considered a blessing. Today it is looked upon as a tragedy. Conscious dying is, in my opinion, the best death.

There is what I refer to as a consciousness theory of relativity. When we sleep the waking state is considered false while the state of sleeping consciousness (dreams) is real. Upon awakening the reverse is true. If we thus acknowledge both of these principles as being cor-rect and transitory, we can be more open to the concept that each transition is part of a continual process and is relative to the other. The effect will be a dismissal of the "I" that shackles relativity. Reality is determined by our ability to be open to experiences. It is only when we begin investigating awareness itself that the true nature of consciousness emerges.

Since our conscious mind is addicted to what it receives from the five senses, the subconscious is brainwashed to be shocked by the very idea of death. Unless the connection with the Higher Self is main-tained, the reality of this transition will retard spiritual growth. As in sleep, we do not know what is real. Dreams can be so powerful as to redirect our lives. Dying can also be a significant impediment or facilitator to our being. Prejudicial attitudes such as "I am the light," or "there is nothing beyond the physical body" merely detour us from the pure and simple state of being.

Even most of those who have had an NDE fail to identify the true nature of the light. This light is our higher self. We must unite with it. Yes, the survivors of NDEs describe how brilliant and beautiful the light is, but none appear to want to merge with it. Herein lies the problem with unconscious dying and this is the main reason I classify all NDEs as unconscious versus conscious dying. Enlightenment can only become manifest when we eliminate this illusion of separateness and merge with this light.

We are born with a highly developed physical brain, yet we use less than one percent of it. The part that we do use is erroneously programmed to suffer and wallow in ignorance. This ignorance creates insecurity, fear, destructiveness, and selfishness. The result is conflict, distrust, competitiveness, war, misery, and unconscious death.

Let me point out that it is not the premeditative purpose of the brain or our five senses to obscure the soul entering into the newborn. The system is created for these structures to assist the soul's spiritual growth. It is the shock of unconscious dying and its subsequent unconscious rebirth that results in our lack of awareness and regression of our true nature.

It is the empowered soul that will find it easier and more rewarding in respect to conscious dying techniques. There are some behaviors that we as living beings can adopt to facilitate spiritual growth and enhance our success in the application of conscious dying techniques. These are:

- Be loving, unselfish, and kind. Love is the most important quality in the universe.

- Be a giver. Eliminate the tendency to take from others. Live a more simple, quality life.

- Reduce your attachment to material possessions. Enjoy them all you want but be willing to lose them without envy, resentment, anger, or other negative emotional responses.

- Be empowered. You may want certain things out of life but never be needy.

- Be God-oriented instead of world-oriented.

- Be humble. Eliminate the desire to be ruthless, aggressive, and conceited. Remove all tendencies to be superficial, vain, and phony.

- Learn not to identify too strongly with your body. Say to yourself, "I am a spiritual soul, immortal and eternal. I create my own reality." The body eventually dies, but the soul is eternal.

Stephen Cummins, a twenty-four-year-old lance-bombardier in the Royal Artillery in Northern Ireland, was one of two soldiers killed when IRA terrorists exploded a land mine under an Army land rover. Shortly before his untimely death, this brave young soldier wrote a poem to his parents. This precognition of his own death contains many poignant points concerning the theme of this book.

> Do not stand at my grave and weep
> I am not there. I do not sleep.
> I am a thousand winds that blow.
> I am the diamond glints on snow.
> I am the sunlight on ripened grain.
> I am the gentle autumn rain.
> When you awaken in the morning's hush
> I am the swift uplifting rush
> of quiet birds in circles flight.
> I am the soft stars that shine at night.
> Do not stand at my grave and cry
> I am not there. I did not die.

GLOSSARY

Absolute Ground: The reality of all things. The universe is only one manifestation of this Absolute. The Absolute Ground is not separated as a type of creator distinct from that which is created. This is a component of the Perennial Philosophy of all religions.

Akashic Records: The record of a soul's past, present, and future lives stored on the causal plane. The soul may tap into these records on any plane, but it is easier to do this when the soul resides on the soul plane.

Angels: Entities of pure spirit who assist humans in time of great stress. Many equate these beings with Masters and Guides. Angels are a component of most religions of the world.

Altered State of Consciousness (ASC): A term describing the alpha brain wave level that is characteristic of hypnosis, meditation, and daydreams, and all out-of-body experiences.

Bardo: The intermediate experiences between physical death and rebirth according to Westerners. The Eastern definition refers to any of six transitory and illusory states of consciousness: waking, dreaming, profound meditation, dying, the reality between lives, and rebirth.

Cleansing: The technique of introducing the subconscious mind and soul to the Higher Self (superconscious mind) so that a connection results. This is also called a superconscious mind tap and Clear Light.

Conscious Dying: The process of maintaining a connection between the soul and the Higher Self at the moment of physical death in order to assure the soul's arrival at the soul plane without the interference of disorienting forces of the karmic cycle. This technique may result in the immediate liberation of the soul from the need to reincarnate.

Conscious Mind Proper: The analytical, critical, and left brain of our mind. Our ego defense mechanisms constitute this part of our consciousness.

Conscious Out-of-Body Experience (COBE): The state of awareness exhibited by the soul when it dies consciously.

Conscious Rebirth: The mechanism of reincarnation characterized by the soul entering a newborn's body without having to experience the disorienting forces of the karmic cycle.

Eucharist: A Christian commemoration or prayer of the deprived soul. This is one of the most ancient of Christian practices.

Higher Self: This is another term describing the superconscious mind or perfect energy component of the soul. The Higher Self is a remnant of the God energy.

Karma: The moral law of cause and effect that states that the individual's present state of being is determined by the soul's past thoughts and actions. These, in turn, influence future lessons to be learned.

Koan: This is a question or problem that appears to be impossible to solve. For example, the question "what is the sound of one hand clapping?" is a Koan. The student solves this by focusing his or her concentration in meditation for several hours. The solution appears in the form of an illuminated perception.

Liberation: The ability of the soul to free itself from the karmic cycle or cycle of birth and death. Enlightenment is also used to describe this process.

Lords of Karma: There are four or seven of these entities who function as cosmic administrators registering all actions and experiences of the soul in the akashic records. These beings, also known as Lipika, then parcel out karmic tests to the soul.

Lucid Dreaming: A type of dream during which the dreamer is aware of being in the dream state. Lucid dreamers are often able to direct the outcome of the dream. This is a type of out-of-body experience.

Masters and Guides: These perfect entities have long since completed their karmic cycle and have chosen to remain on the lower five planes to assist initiated souls in their quest for perfection. Some refer to these beings as angels.

Mystery Schools: The religion practiced by the ancients during which initiates were trained in the art of conscious dying. Mystery Schools have survived throughout history in the form of Freemasonry, the Rosicrucians, Theosophy, and other practices.

Near Death Experience (NDE): A form of out-of-body experience during which the physical body actually dies for a few moments to several minutes before returning back to life. This term was coined by Dr. Raymond Moody.

Nidanas: These are twelve specific forces we create which can be used to keep us within the confines of the karmic cycle or to liberate the soul from this cycle of birth and death.

Out of Body Experience (OBE): These are altered states of consciousness that a soul exhibits whenever it leaves the physical body. Dreams, hypnosis, meditation, times of extreme duress, and NDEs are examples of this phenomenon.

Osiris: The Egyptian god and judge of the dead. He is also their symbol of resurrection. Osiris is the arbiter of the future destiny of man, according to *The Egyptian Book of the Dead*.

Partial Death: A hopelessness exhibited by elderly patients in nursing homes and hospitals. This state of merely existing is accompanied by severe depression.

Perennial Philosophy: A common core to all religions, delineated by Huxley. It is defined as the transcendental essence of all main religions presented through their mystical traditions.

Plane Concept: The paradigm that the universe is divided into three major types of planes. The lower five planes make up the karmic cycle. The sixth or soul plane is where a soul chooses its next life. Finally, there are seven higher planes with the God or nameless plane representing the thirteenth plane. A soul must be liberated from its karmic cycle to be able to travel through the higher planes to God.

Pyramid Texts: Inscribed hieroglyphic characters on the walls of certain pyramids in Egypt. These texts, along with the *Coffin Texts,* make up a good part of the *Egyptian Book of the Dead.*

Soul: The electromagnetic energy (alpha brain wave) that constitutes our very being. This is also called the subconscious mind and it is what reincarnates into a new body when the previous physical body dies.

Subcycles: These are smaller sets of lessons that the soul must learn as part of its total karmic cycle in order to perfect itself. Group karma is exhibited during a subcycle in which for several lifetimes the soul reincarnates with the same collection of other souls.

Superconscious Mind: This is the same as the Higher Self.

Thanatology: The science of death and dying established by the psychiatrist Elizabeth Kübler-Ross.

Unconscious Dying: The process by which a soul fails to maintain a connection with its Higher Self at the moment of death, leaving it exposed to the disorienting forces of the karmic cycle. NDEs are also examples of unconscious dying. Most forms of transitions experienced by souls are unfortunately of this type.

Unconscious Rebirth: The process of a soul entering into a newborn after being exposed to the disorienting forces of the karmic cycle because of its failure to maintain a connection with its Higher Self when it died in its previous life. The great majority of rebirths occurring throughout our society's history have been of this type.

BIBLIOGRAPHY

Arya, Pandit Usharbudh. *Meditation and the Art of Dying.* Honesdale, PA: Himalayan International Institute of Yoga, Science and Philosophy, 1979.

Blofeld, John. *The Tantric Mysticism of Tibet.* Boston: Shambhala, 1987.

Brandon, S. *Judgement of the Dead: The Idea of Life After Death in the Major Religions.* New York: Scribner's, 1969.

Budge, E. A. W. *The Book of the Dead.* London: Longman & Co., 1895.

Castenada Carlos. *Journey to Ixtlan: The Lessons of Don Juan.* New York: Simon & Schuster, 1972.

Choron, Jacques. *Death and Western Thought.* New York: Collier Books, 1963.

Crookall, Robert. *Casebook of Astral Projection.* New York: Citadel Press, Carol Publishing Group, 1973.

_____. *More Astral Projections.* New York: Citadel Press, Carol Publishing Group, 1964.

_____. *The Study and Practice of Astral Projection.* New York: Citadel Press, Carol Publishing Group, 1966.

Doyle, L. J. *Theological Dimensions of the Liturgy.* Trans. W. A. Jurgens. Collegeville, MN: The Liturgical Press, 1976.

Evans-Wentz, W. Y. *The Tibetan Book of the Dead*. Trans. Lama Kazi Dawa-Samdup. New York: Oxford University Press, 1960.

Fortman, Edmund. *The Triune God: A Historical Study of The Doctrine of the Trinity*. Philadelphia: Westminster Publishing, 1972.

Fox, Oliver. *Astral Projection*. London: University Books, 1962.

Franciscan Thomas of Celano. *Dies Irae*. Trans. Ruby Spine. Sag Harbor, NY: Permanent Press, 1990.

Garesche, Rev. Edward, S.J. *Dominican Missal*. Milwaukee: Bruce Publishing Co., 1942.

_____. *Moments With God*. Milwaukee: Bruce Publishing Co., 1942.

Glaser, Berney G., and Anselm L. Strauss. *Awareness of Dying*. Hawthorne, NY: Aldine de Gruyter, 1969.

Golas, Thaddeus. *The Lazy Man's Guide to Enlightenment*. Palo Alto, CA: Seed Center, 1972.

Goldberg, Bruce. *Past Lives—Future Lives*. New York: Ballantine, 1988.

_____. *The Search for Grace: The True Story of Murder and Reincarnation*. St. Paul, MN: Llewellyn Publications, 1997.

_____. *Soul Healing*. St. Paul, MN: Llewellyn Publications, 1996.

Grof and Halifax. *The Human Encounter with Death*. New York: E. P. Dutton, 1972.

_____. *Beyond Death: The Gates of Consciousness*. London: Thames & Hudson, 1980.

Guthrie, W. K. C. *Orpheus and Greek Religion*. Princeton: Princeton University Press, 1993.

Hart, Hornell. "Scientific Survival Research," *Inter. Journal of Parapsychology* 9, 1967: 43–52.

Hoffmann, Banesh, and Helen Dukas. *Albert Einstein, Creator and Rebel*. New York: Plume Books, 1973.

Holck, Frederick. *Death and Eastern Thought: Understanding Death in Eastern Religions and Philosophies*. Nashville: Abingdon Press, 1974.

BIBLIOGRAPHY

Howe, Quincy Jr. *Reincarnation for the Christian*. Wheaton, IL: Theosophical Publishing House, 1987.

Huxley, Aldous. *The Perennial Philosophy*. New York: Ayer Publishing, 1944.

Kapleau, Roshi Philip. *Awakening to Zen: The Teaching of Roshi Philip Kapleau*. New York: Scribner, 1997.

Kübler-Ross, Elizabeth. *On Death and Dying*. New York: Macmillan, 1969.

LaBerge, Stephan. *Lucid Dreaming*. New York: Ballantine, 1986.

Lamerton, Richard. *Care of the Dying*. Westport, CT: Technomic Press, 1976.

Le Goff, Jacques. *The Birth of Purgatory*, trans. Arthur Goldhammer. Chicago: The University of Chicago Press, 1984.

Lee, Jung Young. *Death and Beyond the Eastern Perspective: A Study Based on the Bardo Thödol and the I Ching*. New York: Gordon and Breach, 1974.

LeShan, Lawrence. *The Medium, the Mystic and the Physicist*. New York: Viking Press, 1974.

Moody, Raymond Jr. *Life After Life*. New York: Bantam, 1975.

Monroe, Robert. *Journeys Out of the Body*. New York: Doubleday, 1973.

Newton, Michael. *Journey of Souls*. St. Paul, MN: Llewellyn Publications, 1995.

O'Connell, Rev. John P., and Jex Martin, eds. *The Prayer Book*. Chicago: The Catholic Press, 1954.

Pattison, E. Mansell. *The Experience of Dying*. Englewood Cliffs, NJ: Prentice-Hall, 1991.

Perkins, James. *Through Death to Rebirth*. Wheaton, IL: Theosophical Publishing House, 1974.

Plato. *Euthyphro* in *A Guided Tour of Five Works of Plato*. Mountain View, CA: Mayfield Publishing Co., 1988.

Premananda, Swami. *Katha Upanishad: Dialogue of Death and Vision of Immortality*. Washington, DC: Self Realization Fellowship, 1943.

BIBLIOGRAPHY

Ring, Kenneth. *Life at Death: A Scientific Investigation of the Near-Death Experience.* New York: Quill, 1982.

Ritchie, G. *My Life After Dying.* Norfolk, VA: Hampton Roads Publishing Co., 1991.

Sabom, Michael. *Recollections of Death: A Medical Investigation.* New York: Harper & Row, 1982.

Shneidman, Edwin. *Death: Current Perspectives.* Palo Alto, CA: Mayfield Publishing Co., 1984.

Steiner, Rudolf. *Life Between Death and Rebirth.* Trans. R. M. Querido. New York: Anthroposophic Press, 1968.

Swedenborg, Emanuel. *Compendium of the Theological and Spiritual Writings of Emanuel Swedenborg.* Boston: Crosby and Nichols, 1853.

Verney, Thomas, with John Kelly. *The Secret Life of the Unborn Child.* New York: Summit Books, 1981.

Wilber, Ken, ed. *The Holographic Paradigm and Other Paradoxes.* Boulder, CO: Shambhala Publications, 1982.

Wolf, Fred Alan. *The Body Quantum: The New Physics of Body, Mind and Health.* New York: Macmillan Pub. Co., 1986.

INDEX

A

Absolute Ground, 54, 221

Altered states of consciousness, 8, 10, 33, 57, 223

Angels, 19–21, 44–47, 101, 104, 194–195, 202, 205–208, 221, 223

B

Blavatsky, Madame H. P., 209

C

Christ, Jesus, 17, 33, 87, 153, 189–191, 195–196

Christian Masses, 189, 191, 193, 195, 197

Cleansing, i, ix, 8, 25–27, 123, 125, 127–128, 151, 179, 222

Conscious dying, ix, 3–5, 7–9, 11, 16, 19, 23, 25–27, 29–30, 32, 35–37, 39–42, 48, 52–54, 57, 60, 65, 68–69, 71, 79, 83, 85–87, 89, 91, 93–97, 99–100, 105–106, 110, 115–116, 121, 123–132, 134–135, 137–139, 146–147, 149, 151–155, 157, 199, 214, 217–219, 222–223

Conscious mind proper, 7, 86, 216, 222

Conscious out-of-body experience, i, x, 3, 8, 11, 53, 95, 134, 137, 151, 222

Conscious rebirth, 11, 91, 115–116, 118–119, 132, 222

Crookall, Robert, 72, 76, 225

E

Egyptian Book of the Dead, i, 26, 152, 167, 169-171, 173, 175, 190, 192, 223-224

Einstein, Albert, 61, 64–66, 226

Eucharist, 191–192, 222

Stay in Touch. . .

Llewellyn publishes hundreds of books on your favorite subjects

On the following pages you will find listed some books now available on related subjects. Your local bookstore stocks most of these and will stock new Llewellyn titles as they become available. We urge your patronage.

Order by Phone

Call toll-free within the U.S. and Canada, **1–800–THE MOON**.
In Minnesota call **(612) 291–1970**.
We accept Visa, MasterCard, and American Express.

Order by Mail

Send the full price of your order (MN residents add 7% sales tax) in U.S. funds to:

> **Llewellyn Worldwide**
> **P.O. Box 64383, Dept. K319–2**
> **St. Paul, MN 55164–0383, U.S.A.**

Postage and Handling

- • $4.00 for orders $15.00 and under
- • $5.00 for orders over $15.00
- • No charge for orders over $100.00

We ship UPS in the continental United States. We cannot ship to P.O. boxes. Orders shipped to Alaska, Hawaii, Canada, Mexico, and Puerto Rico will be sent first-class mail.

International orders: Airmail—add freight equal to price of each book to the total price of order, plus $5.00 for each non-book item (audiotapes, etc.); Surface mail—add $1.00 per item.

Allow 4–6 weeks delivery on all orders. Postage and handling rates subject to change.

Group Discounts

We offer a 20% quantity discount to group leaders or agents. You must order a minimum of 5 copies of the same book to get our special quantity price.

Free Catalog

Get a free copy of our color catalog, *New Worlds of Mind and Spirit*. Subscribe for just $10.00 in the United States and Canada ($20.00 overseas, first-class mail). Many bookstores carry *New Worlds*—ask for it!

SOUL HEALING

Dr. Bruce Goldberg

George: overcame lung cancer and a life of smoking through hypnotic programming.

Mary: tripled her immune system's response to AIDS with the help of age progression.

Now you, too, can learn to raise the vibrational rate of your soul (or subconscious mind) to stimulate your body's own natural healing processes. Explore several natural approaches to healing that include past life regression and future life progression, hypnotherapy, soulmates, angelic healing, near-death experiences, shamanic healing, acupuncture, meditation, yoga, and the new physics.

The miracle of healing comes from within. After reading *Soul Healing*, you will never view your life and the universe in the same way again.

1-56718-317-4, 304 pp., 6 x 9, softcover   **$14.95**

THE SEARCH FOR GRACE
The True Story of Murder & Reincarnation

Dr. Bruce Goldberg

The true story of murder and reincarnation featured as a "CBS Movie of the Week"

THE SEARCH FOR GRACE?

"The best documented case of reincarnation."
—*from the introduction by Brad Steiger*

DR. BRUCE GOLDBERG

An unsolved murder mystery on the books since 1927 ... one modern woman's obsession with an abusive lover ... and a karmic journey that winds through a maze of past lives—all of these unite into the *best*-documented case of reincarnation in the Western world.

The Search for Grace is the true story of Ivy, a 26-year-old pharmacist who sought the help of Dr. Bruce Goldberg to put a stop to her inexplainable attraction to John, her physically and psychologically abusive boyfriend. Under hypnosis, she discovered that John had been her lover—and her murderer—in 20 of her 46 past lives.

When Ivy recounts the details of her 46th life as roaring-twenties party girl Grace Doze, hypnotherapy and real-life dovetail into a dramatic twist of fate. It was May 19, 1927, when the body of Grace Doze turned up in a Buffalo, N.Y., creek. Her murder remained a mystery until 60 years later, when Dr. Goldberg put Ivy into a superconscious state, and Grace's true killer was brought to light for the world to see.

1-56718-318-2, 6 x 9, 288 pp., photos, softcover　　　　　　**$12.95**

To order by phone, call 1–800–THE–MOON
Prices subject to change without notice.

A PRACTICAL GUIDE TO PAST LIFE REGRESSION

Florence Wagner McClain

Florence Wagner McClain

Have you ever felt that there had to be more to life than this? Have you ever met someone and felt an immediate kinship? Have you ever visited a strange place and felt that you had been there before? Have you struggled with frustrations and fears which seem to have no basis in your present life? Are you afraid of death? Have you ever been curious about reincarnation or maybe just interested enough to be skeptical?

This book presents a simple technique that you can use to obtain past life information *today*. There are no mysterious preparations, no groups to join, no philosophy to which you must adhere. You don't even have to believe in reincarnation. The tools are provided for you to make your own investigations, find your own answers and make your own judgements as to the validity of the information and its usefulness to you.

Whether you believe in reincarnation or not, past life regression remains a powerful and valid tool for self-exploration. Information procured through this procedure can be invaluable for personal growth and inner healing, no matter what its source. Florence McClain's guidebook is an eminently sane and capable guide for those who wish to explore their possible past lives or conduct regressions themselves.

0-87542-510-0, 160 pp., 5 ¼ x 8, softcover   **$7.95**

JOURNEY OF SOULS
Case Studies of Life Between Lives

Michael Newton, Ph.D.

This remarkable book uncovers—for the first time—the mystery of life in the spirit world after death on earth. Dr. Michael Newton, a hypnotherapist in private practice, has developed his own hypnosis technique to reach his subjects' hidden memories of the hereafter. The narrative is woven as a progressive travel log around the accounts of twenty-nine people who were placed in a state of superconsciousness. While in deep hypnosis, these subjects describe what has happened to them between their former reincarnations on earth. They reveal graphic details about how it feels to die, who meets us right after death, what the spirit world is really like, where we go and what we do as souls, and why we choose to come back in certain bodies.

After reading *Journey of Souls,* you will acquire a better understanding of the immortality of the human soul. Plus, you will meet day-to-day personal challenges with a greater sense of purpose as you begin to understand the reasons behind events in your own life.

1-56718-485-5, 288 pp., 6 x 9, softcover   **$12.95**

ENTERING THE SUMMERLAND
Customs and Rituals of Transition into the Afterlife

Edain McCoy

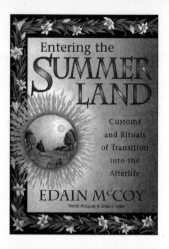

All of us must face it sooner or later—the devastating loss of a loved one. For Pagans, the period of mourning can be especially trying, simply because many are isolated from a community which shares their spiritual viewpoint of death and the afterlife.

Unlike the mainstream religions, paganism has had no written guide specifically designed to offer comfort and direction to the bereaved—until now. *Entering the Summerland* fills this need by providing rituals for healing and passing, as well as practical ideas about dealing with grief. *Entering the Summerland* builds concepts and ideas about death into a framework for open discussion, ritual structure, funeral planning, and bereavement support. It also attempts to legitimize griefs that are not yet acceptable to the larger society in which we live, such as mourning the loss of a pet or a familiar.

1–56718–665–3, 256 pp., 7 x 10, illus., softcover   **$17.95**

HOW TO UNCOVER YOUR
PAST LIVES

Ted Andrews

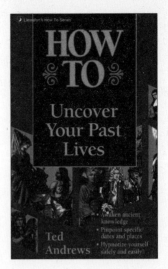

Knowledge of your past lives can be extremely rewarding. It can assist you in opening to new depths within your own psychological makeup. It can provide greater insight into present circumstances with loved ones, career, and health. It is also a lot of fun.

Now Ted Andrews shares with you nine different techniques that you can use to access your past lives. Between techniques, Andrews discusses issues such as karma and how it is expressed in your present life; the source of past life information; soul mates and twin souls; proving past lives; the mysteries of birth and death; animals and reincarnation; abortion and pre-mature death; and the role of reincarnation in Christianity.

To explore your past lives, you need only use one or more of the techniques offered. Complete instructions are provided for a safe and easy regression. Learn to dowse to pinpoint the years and places of your lives with great accuracy, make your own self-hypnosis tape, attune to the incoming child during pregnancy, use the tarot and the cabala in past life meditations, keep a past life journal and more.

0-87542-022-2, 240 pp., mass market, illus.   **$4.99**

To order by phone, call 1–800–THE–MOON
Prices subject to change without notice.

TRUE HAUNTINGS
Spirits with a Purpose

Hazel M. Denning, Ph.D.

Do spirits feel and think? Does death automatically promote them to a paradise—or as some believe, a hell? Real-life ghostbuster Dr. Hazel M. Denning reveals the answers through case histories of the friendly and hostile earthbound spirits she has encountered. Learn the reasons spirits remain entrapped in the vibrational force field of the earth: fear of going to the other side, desire to protect surviving loved ones, and revenge.

Dr. Denning also shares fascinating case histories involving spirit possession, psychic attack, mediumship and spirit guides. Find out why spirits haunt us in *True Hauntings*, the only book of its kind written from the perspective of the spirits themselves.

1-56718-218-6, 240 pp., 6 x 9, index, glossary, softcover $12.95

HOW TO MEET & WORK WITH SPIRIT GUIDES

Ted Andrews

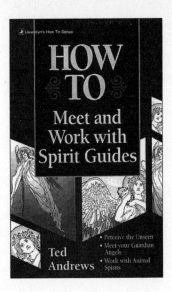

We often experience spirit contact in our lives but fail to recognize it for what it is. Now you can learn to access and attune to beings such as guardian angels, nature spirits and elementals, spirit totems, archangels, gods and goddesses—as well as family and friends after their physical death.

Contact with higher soul energies strengthens the will and enlightens the mind. Through a series of simple exercises, you can safely and gradually increase your awareness of spirits and your ability to identify them. You will learn to develop an intentional and directed contact with any number of spirit beings. Discover meditations to open up your subconscious. Learn which acupressure points effectively stimulate your intuitive faculties. Find out how to form a group for spirit work, use crystal balls, perform automatic writing, attune your aura for spirit contact, use sigils to contact the great archangels and much more! Read How to Meet and Work with Spirit Guides and take your first steps through the corridors of life beyond the physical.

0–87542–008–7, 192 pp., mass market, illus.   **$4.99**

To order by phone, call 1–800–THE–MOON
Prices subject to change without notice.

THE POWER OF DREAMING
Messages from Your Inner Self

D. Jason Cooper

Unlock the secret of your dreams and open the door to your inner self! Our dreams hold a wisdom which can guide us, protect us and better our lives, if we listen to it. *The Power of Dreaming* presents a new, reliable and effective "technology" for interpreting your dreams, as it is the first book to separate dream symbols from their context to better interpret each element: the nature of the dream and your role within it; its events, people and objects; archetypes in the dream; and the dream's class (whether it's a problem-solving dream, a house-cleaning dream, a psychological dream or an occult dream). Once you string meanings of all these elements together, you'll arrive at a complete, accurate and insightful interpretation of your dreams. This brand-new technique illustrates how events, rather than objects, are the key to unlocking your dreams' meanings. Includes three different dream dictionaries: one to interpret the meaning of events, one for objects and one for archetypes.

The Power of Dreaming gives you all the information you need to follow a program of self-knowledge and understanding through your dreams. Take this fascinating road to self-discovery every night!

1-56718-175-9, 224 pp., 6 x 9, softcover   **$12.00**

THE ULTIMATE CURE
The Healing Energy Within You

Dr. Jim Dreaver

The Ultimate Cure will open a door into consciousness and literally bring you into a direct, first-hand experience of illumination—an experience that will stimulate your mind, warm your heart, and feed your soul.

Dr. Jim Dreaver provides a first-hand account of the spiritual journey and outlines the steps needed to live in the world with an authentic sense of wisdom, love and power. He addresses the issues of meditation, work as a spiritual exercise, harnessing the power of the mind, conscious breathing, and healing the wounds of the past. Dr. Dreaver's main theme is that spiritual presence, which is the source of all healing, is an actual, palpable reality that can be felt and tapped into.

To realize enlightenment, you must have a tremendous hunger for it. This delightfully honest and wonderfully human book will stimulate your appetite and, by the time you turn to the last page, will leave you feeling totally satisfied.

1-56718-244-5, 288 pp., 6 x 9, softcover   **$14.95**

To order by phone, call 1–800–THE–MOON
Prices subject to change without notice.

POWER
The Power to Create the Future

Eric Mitchell

Each of us has something special about us. Each of us has a unique vision, a meaning and purpose to our life, with which we can be the most successful, the most fulfilled, and the most happy. The discovery and fulfillment of that unique vision is your life purpose and will bring with it your highest material fulfillment.

Power is the first book to reveal how to contact, communicate, and work with the highest spiritual power and how to make that power available for the spiritual and material transformation of the individual and the world.

Twenty years of Eric Mitchell's spiritual quest have been synthesized into less than 200 pages, so that every student of spirituality and life can find here a treasure trove of wisdom and its practical use. These are directions to find your true home, the One Power. The great spiritual beings of the past changed our societies, but the transformation of human consciousness did not happen. This book presents a new approach to solving that problem.

087542-499-6, 192 pp., mass market, illus.   **$3.95**

To order by phone, call 1–800–THE—MOON
Prices subject to change without notice.

CREATE YOUR OWN JOY
A Guide for Transforming Your Life

Elizabeth Jean Rogers

Uncover the wisdom, energy and love of your higher self and discover the peace and joy for which you yearn! This highly structured journal-workbook is designed to guide you through the process of understanding how you create your own joy by how you choose to respond to people and situations in your life.

Each chapter offers guided meditations on overcoming blocks—such as guilt, grief, fear and destructive behavior—that keep happiness from you; thoughtful questions to help you focus your feelings; concrete suggestions for action; and affirmations to help you define and fulfill your deepest desires and true needs. As you record your responses to the author's questions, you will transform this book into a personal expression of your own experience.

Life is too short to waste your energy on negative thoughts and emotions—use the uncomplicated, dynamic ideas in this book to get a fresh outlook on current challenges in your life, and open the door to your joyful higher self.

1-56718-354-9, 240 pp., 6 x 9, illus., softcover   **$10.00**